Moms $aving Money

The Tightwad Twins

ANN FOX CHODAKOWSKI & SUSAN FOX WOOD

HARVEST HOUSE PUBLISHERS
Eugene, Oregon 97402

Cover by Terry Dugan Design, Minneapolis, Minnesota

MOMS SAVING MONEY
Copyright © 2000 by Ann Fox Chodakowski and Susan Fox Wood
Published by Harvest House Publishers
Eugene, Oregon 97402

Library of Congress Cataloging-in-Publication Data

Chodakowski, Ann Fox, 1952-
   Moms saving money / Ann Fox Chodakowski and Susan Fox Wood
        p.   cm.
   ISBN 0-7369-0200-7
   1. Finance, Personal.   2. Saving and investment.   3. Home
 economics.   I. Wood, Susan Fox. 1952- . II. Title.
HG179.F667 2000
332.024--dc21   99-41566
                                                                      CIP

Printed in the United States of America.

                00 01 02 03 04 05 06 / BP / 10 9 8 7 6 5 4 3 2 1

This book is dedicated foremost to God for the sustaining grace and sense of strength He has always given us to carry on!

We also dedicate it to our agent, Greg Johnson, of Alive Communications for his never failing belief in us from the very start, as well as to Becky Freeman, our editing angel, who pulled us through some tight deadlines and helped us compile our childhood memory stories.

And we mustn't forget our present family members who endured many fast-food nights while we were writing this book.

And, of course, to our tightwad Mama and Daddy who showed us the way to the best of all gifts—the free gift of eternal life.

We extend our gratitude to our big sis, Charlotte Fox Messmer of Williamsburg, VA. She contributed many of her recipes and cooking tips. She is a gifted cook, and we're jealous of her! Thank you, Char, for always being there for us.

We also want to thank our readers who have given us tips that made their lives easier or more organized. You shared your best ideas with us, and now we're passing them on to help women everywhere.

Contents

The Tightwad Twins

The Tightwad Twins

Many people have asked how we began calling ourselves The Tightwad Twins, making a viable career out of being incredibly cheap. Here's the story.

With Susan still living in Paducah, and me in Tampa, we logged in many an hour chatting over the phone (at off-peak rates, needless to say). During one of those phone conversations, we laughed about our obsession with saving, teasingly calling ourselves Tightwad Twins—and the name stuck! Our present husbands (yes, God blessed us with second chances at marriage!) saw our knack for thriftiness and encouraged us to write down our best tips. We put together a huge book of tips (photocopied!), and offered it for sale in various ads via an 800 number. We got lots of local press for our venture, and when the Associated Press picked up the story, orders began pouring in.

Then we called a national talk show and offered ourselves as the perfect human interest guests. We wore T-shirts with our 800 number blazoned across the front (of course) on the show, and by the time we got home, we had more orders waiting for us.

"Were you nervous?" our friends asked. We know it sounds strange, but we've never been the least bit afraid to be on TV or to speak in front of others. We believe everything that has happened to us is a gift from God, and we are excited to share what we've learned. It's truly like being rewarded for having been poor for so long!

Soon after an appearance on "The Maury Povich Show," we found our wonderful literary agent, Greg Johnson, who helped us sell our first book to a big publisher. Though we haven't exactly jumped from being Poor-and-Unknown to Rich-and-Famous, our lives have definitely taken an interesting and profitable turn. And now, with a new publisher, we've written another book! We share this story, not to brag on ourselves, but as living proof that if we can find creative solutions to life's financial challenges, *you* can.

One of the nicest surprises of suddenly finding ourselves mini-celebrities is receiving fan mail and phone calls from fellow Tightwadettes. We realized from the beginning of this venture that there would be some women who just wouldn't "get us." But if you and your spouse are having trouble making ends meet, or you've quit your outside job to stay home with your kids (and have to live on half of your previous family income), or you're a single parent trying to raise children on your own, or you're just starting out on your own, or you just appreciate the challenge of living cheaply— we're here to help. Let's jump into tightwad paradise!

Family Album

A Double Batch of Babies

From the time we were old enough to lick the spoon, our budget-wise mother told us we could save time and money by doubling recipes. Even at that young age we wondered if Mama had somehow bargained with God, asking Him for a double batch of babies just to save money on the doctor bill. Whatever the case, we entered the world as "two-fers."

It was a cold January night in 1952 when Susan and I (Ann)* were born to William and Imogene Fox in the sleepy, quaint southern town of Paducah, Kentucky. Susan was born first and I followed next, bottom and feet first.

---

* Susan and Ann coauthored this book, but sometimes Ann will introduce a ...chapter and sometimes Susan will. Since Ann is the "bossiest" twin, we voted that she go first!

Though Susan was the first to make the grand entrance into the world, she claims that I actually pushed her out because I tend to be the "pushy" twin. We were preemies, born at seven months gestation, weighing in at five pounds apiece.

Our big sister, Char, at age ten, was thrilled to have two live "dolls" to play with, diaper, rock, and mother. Brother Jim, then age seven, found himself suddenly surrounded by females. He's still in a bit of shock. Life as Jim knew it would never be the same again because the "Fox House" was now a henhouse of crying, cackling girls.

Two more babies also meant two more mouths to feed. An already tight budget had to be stretched even more. Money was scarce and work was hard, yet our parents, William and Imogene, managed to leave us a legacy of love, laughter, and creativity. We kids never guessed we were poor. Indeed we felt rich. We were not only lavished with love and attention, we were often told of our value to God—and of His generosity to us. Whenever we ventured a complaint about our lack, Mama would tell us stories of children starving in exotic foreign lands. How grateful they would be for a warm bowl of oatmeal or potato soup. "Now girls," we can almost hear her say, "just pretend for a moment that we're a missionary family out on the plains of Africa. No stores, no electric lights—just giraffe and hippopotamus meat to eat. Now, aren't you happy for all that we've got?"

Perhaps because we weren't materially wealthy, we've always taken extra pleasure in life's smallest gifts. Mama's soup filled with garden veggies simmering on the stove. The fresh smell of sun-warmed sheets just in from the clothesline. A cookie jar filled with fresh oatmeal raisin confections that covered Mama's "stash." (Who needed a fancy bank for depositing savings when you had a perfectly good cookie jar right there on the kitchen counter?)

We probably also owe our wacky sense of humor to our Mama, who could laugh as easily as she could bake a pie from scratch. She especially loved cutting out cartoons and quips from newspapers and magazines. Now we can't read an amusing anecdote without passing it on to our siblings. How can you not share a laugh? It's free and it's cheap, and it does everyone good!

Our precious Mama passed away much too soon. She was only 52 when she died of cancer, showing incredible peace through it all. She was the spiritual rock of our family. When she was gone, we thought our lives were over and wondered how our hearts would ever mend. But we grew up, got married, had children, struggled, and then one day we found ourselves twin single mothers. During those difficult days of emotional and financial survival, we would remember our parents' tightwad ways.

> *You never know the value of water*
> *until the well runs dry.*

Often we'd call each other on the phone with some memory of Mama's homespun wisdom or a recollection of how she'd stretched a pound of hamburger to feed a party of 12. Then we began collecting our own tightwad discoveries and writing them down. One day we realized, we have a ball being cheap! Why not share this with other busy moms?

So we put thousands of tips to paper, got ourselves on radio and television, met a fancy publisher who noticed our crazy, fun message of frugal living and published our first book. Well, the rest is "sistory." We soon dubbed ourselves "The Tightwad Twins," and basically we hope to end our tale living happily (and cheaply) ever after.

With thankful hearts we offer up this guide for "survival of the cheapest." We've also included bits of homespun wisdom and humor to spice things up a bit. By the time you have closed the last page, we hope you have discovered, as we have, how to double the fun in frugality and life!

Tightwad Family Album

Daddy and Mama Fox

We never thought we were poor. Indeed, Daddy and Mama, made us feel rich—in love, laughter, and creativity.

To save money on a hairdresser, Mama cut our bangs herself. We wonder if she used a dog's hind leg as a pattern.

"We were 'two-fers' from the day we were born..."

Our budget-wise, creative Mama made detachable white collars and aprons to be used with many of our homemade dresses. She also cut the toes out of our outgrown, black Sunday shoes and made "sandals"!

A year never went by without one of Mama's Toni home permanents.

"Our minds are filled with memories of the past. We have choices about which memories we pull out and rerun across the screens of our minds."

—Carol Kuykendall,
A Mother's Footprints of Faith

Poor Charlotte suffered perhaps more than the rest of us younger kids. As the oldest, she saw her life change dramatically when we were born. Char was quite a seamstress, and she made all of her own clothes as a teenager. In this photo she's wearing the prom dress she made when she was 15!

Our big brother, Jim. Dad built a playhouse for us out of scrap lumber, old windows, and discarded shingles. We loved it until our brother used it as a clubhouse and burned a hole in one of the pieces of furniture. He is an attorney today. We're still mad at him.

2

Mama's Hot Apple Pie—
In a Hurry!

Cost-Cutting, Time-Saving, Mouthwatering
Recipes and Shopping Tips

After Mama was gone, we girls (Charlotte, Ann, and Susan) began to view every item Mama touched and used as a treasure, especially her work-worn cookbook. In leafing through it, the word "comfort food" took on new meaning. We can whip up a batch of Mama's homemade bread or her hot apple pie and be immediately transported on aromas of vanilla and spice to the kitchen haven of our childhood. Oh, the memories one simple piece of food can bring to mind!

Our mama always tried to have meat for every meal. Even if all she could produce was a half piece of bacon each, it counted as our "protein portion." How good that piece of smoky, crisp pork tasted on a chilly school morning. To this day, all four of us grown children crave bacon and can't ever seem to get enough of it!

Mama made kitchen chores fun, turning a simple task like snapping beans and shelling peas into an art form. We each had a designated spot on the back porch come shellin' time. There was a big metal pot for the whole beans, one for the scraps, and one for the finished pea product. To the rhythm of "snap, pull, peel, plop" we would sit and talk with our Mama about school or friends or the meaning of life, stopping only to visit with the neighbors as they passed by. "Shellin' Peas Therapy," it was to us.

> *The biggest sellers in any bookstore are the cookbooks and the diet books. The cookbooks tell you how to prepare the food, and the diet books tell you not to eat any of it.*

Trips to the Farmers Market were one of the highlights of our week—and of our childhood. We always stopped on the way to town at the corner drug store/soda fountain in Paducah. There, we were allowed to choose any flavor of ice cream—one scoop only. Today, as we lick the sticky sweetness of delicious ice cream with gusto, we all remember the quiet, satisfied smile on our Mama's face.

One day, not long after Mama died, we were poring through her cookbook when Susan suddenly said, "Oh, my..."

"Oh my—what?" Charlotte and I asked in unison.

"Oh, my," Susan echoed to herself, this time with a catch in her voice. "Read this. It was tucked in between Apple Pies and Bread Pudding." Susan gently handed us a slip of yellowed paper, which had obviously been cut out and placed in the cookbook with care. It was a little anecdote by Marjorie Holmes entitled "The Lightest Blanket."

> "Do mothers sleep?" your little boy asks.
>
> "Certainly, why?"
>
> "Well, whenever anybody calls you in the night you always come."
>
> Sleep—do mothers ever truly sleep?...Surely sleep is the lightest blanket that a mother pulls over herself. And however deeply she burrows into its comfort, another self perches on the rim of consciousness, alert and on guard.
>
> Let a child cry out, cough, even kick off his covers and be cold and the signal is flashed.
>
> Like a fish striking for the fly, she darts to the surface without even considering. She's out of bed and down the hall, heading unerringly for the proper child.
>
> "Yes, you smile, remembering how your mother would appear with the same mystifying promptness out of the dark. "Mothers sleep, too. But not very soundly."

It was as if Mama had left us a buried treasure between "How to Make a Perfect Pie Crust" and "Fool Proof Gravy." It was a reminder that no matter how far away it seemed our mother was, in heaven she was always in a place full of light and joy. And we believe she is watching over us as we go about our days, as we work and mother her grandchildren and shop and stir and try to make the best of what life hands us.

Here is our Mama's treasured recipe for apple pie:

Old-Fashioned Apple Pie

Filling
3 lbs. Granny Smith or Macintosh apples
¼ c. brown sugar
¼ c. white sugar
¼ c. flour
1 tsp. cinnamon
½ tsp. nutmeg
4 T. butter
Peel, core, and slice apples. Mix with rest of ingredients except for butter. Pour into crust.

Crust
2 c. flour
⅔ c. plus 2 T. shortening
1 tsp. salt
2½ T. water (or more if looks too dry)

Divide crust in half. Roll out on floured board, then place in bottom of pie plate. Pour in apple mixture, putting the four tablespoons of butter on top. Roll out the other half of the crust and put it on top of apple mixture. Pinch the crusts together at edges of pie plate. Cut slits in crust top and brush the top of the crust, but not the edges, with canned milk. Bake at 425° for 35 to 40 minutes or until crust is brown and apples are tender.

Now, here's our version.

The Twins' Apple-Pie-in-a-Hurry!

In a bowl, microwave a chopped apple, a marshmallow, and a sprinkle of cinnamon until soft. Sprinkle with crumbled anything: nuts, leftover cookies, buttered breadcrumbs from the morning toast, or that last bit of crackers or cereal at the bottom of the box that none of the kids will eat. Enjoy!

As you can see, though we loved our mother's cooking, our lives (as those of most moms we know) have been set on the fast-forward button. So we've had to simplify most things we learned, including the process of getting food on the table. Between us, we've learned a lot of secrets to creating tasty fare with a minimum of prep time—and we manage to save a buck while we're at it. So now, without further adieu, heeeeeeeeeeeeere's our best cheap kitchen tips and recipes!

5 Keys to Saving Money at the Grocery Store

Menu planning. Plan meals based on what you have on hand in your refrigerator or cupboards. Also plan for snacks and school lunches.

Organization. Organizing your refrigerator and cupboards—and even your freezer—is a must. You should be able to tell in one quick glance what items you need to replenish.

Nevers. Never go shopping hungry or without a grocery list. Never go to the store more than once a week if you can possibly help it!

Eternal grocery list. Keep a perpetual list of foods your family consistently uses. Make several copies, then all you have to do is place a check by what you need. Some stores even have a list you can copy. This helps eliminate impulse purchases and serves as a prompter for items you may otherwise forget to buy.

Yearly special events and holidays. Keep a lookout for specials on these items every grocery trip. Look at unique food containers as well. That red lid olive jar, emptied, would look great filled with Christmas candy and tied with a red ribbon at holiday time. Watch for after-holiday sales, and put those items away in your gift closet or storage space until the seasons roll around again.

Here are some of our favorite tried and true recipes—quick, easy, and most important of all—cheap! Serving size for these recipes is usually for four. If you think the four main food groups are canned, boxed, frozen, and takeout, then these recipes are for you! Rest assured—the Tightwad Twins have dutifully tried out these recipes. It was such a chore! And by the way, don't be afraid to take a break every once in a while. If you are to busy too cook and laugh at the idea of cooking from scratch, then collect those fast-food coupons during the week. Choose the healthiest items on the menu, then eat outside on a picnic table so you won't have a mess to clean up.

> *"We don't mind the rat race, but we could do with a little more cheese."*

Salads
Cool Chicken Salad

    2 c. cooked chicken, chopped (may use turkey)
    1 c. green grapes, chopped
    ½ to 1 c. salad dressing or mayonnaise (according to taste)
    ½ c. thinly sliced onion (red adds color, but any kind will do)
    1 T. lemon juice
    pinch of basil
    lettuce leaves

Mix all ingredients together except lettuce. Serve on the large lettuce leaves.

Chef Salad

    8 oz. jar of soft cheese spread
    ½ c. sour cream
    green onions

1 lb. ham, diced (may use turkey or chicken)
4 hard-boiled eggs, diced
lettuce leaves
shredded cheese

Mix all ingredients together except lettuce and shredded cheese. Serve on lettuce and top with shredded cheese.

Cottage Cheese Salad

1 c. cottage cheese
1 envelope dry onion soup mix
3 T. sour cream
½ tsp. salt
dash of garlic power
mixed veggies—fresh or
canned
¼ c. chopped ripe olives
large green peppers, seeded and hulled

Mix together everything except green peppers. Place in green peppers and serve.

General Meals
Liz Higgs' Famous Casserole

Make at your own risk!

Mix everything on the left side of the fridge with everything on the right side. Cover with potato chips and bake until done.

Vegetable Deluxe

Any bag of frozen vegetables
1 can corn soup
½ c. milk
Shredded cheese
Meat (optional)

Combine, then heat. (Chunks of leftover chicken, turkey, or ham would be a tasty addition.) Garnish with shredded cheese and serve.

Beefy Vegetables

1 bag of frozen vegetables or leftover vegetables
1 can of vegetable beef soup

Combine and heat. Serve over cooked rice.

Note: You don't have to eat meat every day. Try high protein substitutes like beans, rice, pasta, and vegetable casseroles.

Green Bean Casserole

3 cans of french-cut green beans
1 can cream of mushroom soup
dried onion rings or cracker crumbs

Mix together everything except onion rings/cracker crumbs, and cook in casserole dish at 350° for 30 minutes. Add dried onion rings or cracker crumbs and brown another 10 minutes. Serve.

> **Holiday Hint:** *For a neat centerpiece, layer cucumber slices in the shape of a Christmas tree and add small cherry tomatoes for decorations.*

Pasta/Meat Primavera

Macaroni (corkscrew or elbow)
1 can cream of chicken soup
½ c. milk
¼ c. Parmesan cheese
salt and pepper
2 carrots, cooked, or 1 can of carrots
leftover chicken or turkey

Mix together then add cooked and drained macaroni. Heat and serve.

Turkey Bake

1 can cream of celery soup
⅓ c. water
dash of soy sauce
sliced green onions
canned or frozen vegetables
cubed turkey or chicken
rice or noodles

Combine ingredients except rice/noodles in a casserole dish and bake at 350° for 25 minutes. Cook rice or noodles per package instructions. Remove casserole from oven. Stir and add french-fried onions. Serve over rice or noodles.

Simple Vegetable Soup

2 cans vegetable broth (clear)
pinch of garlic powder
pinch of basil
1 can whole, peeled tomatoes
1 can mixed vegetables
1 c. cooked, drained, corkscrew macaroni

Mix together and heat. Serves 6.

Quickie Grilled Cheese Sandwich

sliced bread (white, wheat, or french-sliced)
Pam cooking oil spray
cheese
onions
tomatoes
peppers

Place sliced bread on a cookie sheet slightly sprayed with Pam. Place cheese on bread and add, if desired, onions, tomatoes, and peppers. Bake approximately 15 minutes at 300° or until cheese is melted. Serve with a salad.

Fast Break at Breakfast

cooked rice
sugar
milk
crumbled bacon or sausage, cooked
butter
bananas or other fruit

Mix cooked rice, sugar, crumbled bacon/sausage, and butter together. Add fruit and milk. Heat and serve.

This can be prepared in bulk (without the milk) and kept in the refrigerator. Add milk and heat. This is a wonderful fast breakfast from the fridge.

Hint: Sprinkle wheat germ on hot or cold cereal for an extra nutrition boost.

Tasty Toothpick Meals

Kids love this fun, easy way to serve lunch or dinner!

Wieners or sausage
carrots and other veggies
fruit chunks
tater tots

Slice wieners or sausage. On a Lazy Susan or tray, arrange cooked, bite-sized carrots, other vegetables, and fruit chunks. Let the kids pick and choose and eat with their toothpicks. Serve with tater tots.

Note: Don't forget—fancy colored toothpicks will make your meal extra special and festive.

Fantastic Pita Sandwiches

chicken or turkey salad
fruit
hard-boiled eggs
ruffly lettuce
pita bread

Cut pita bread in half (they'll look like small fans). Stuff with ruffly lettuce leaves then fill them with chicken or turkey salad. Serve with fruit and hard-boiled eggs.

Tooty Fruity Pizza

pizza crust mix or ready-made crust
seasoned tomato or pizza sauce
canned fruit
shredded cheddar cheese

Make the pizza crust as directed. Spread on seasoned tomato sauce or pizza sauce. Drain fruit and place on sauce. Cook until the pizza crust is done (see mix directions). Add shredded cheese for the last 10 minutes or so of baking. Cut and serve.

Yummy and cheap and great for breakfast. Or, for dinner, add cooked, drained hamburger, slices of polish sausage, or pepperoni. Bake in the oven until cheese melts and crust is light brown.

Cheapie Pizza Sandwiches

1 cheese pizza
1 pizza–your choice
pizza or tomato sauce
onions
pepperoni, polish sausage, or hamburger

Buy two cheap pizzas Add to one of the pizzas: extra sauce, onion, and pepperoni, polish sausage slices, or hamburger. Cook both pizzas as directed. Place the plain cheese pizza on top of the other with the crust side up. *Ta-dum!* Pizza sandwiches. Pretty good—and pretty cheap!

Pizzas in a Bowl

canned biscuit dough
pizza or tomato sauce
meat (cooked)
cheese

Optional
onions
peppers
seasonings

Press each biscuit into a bowl-like shape. Place on a cookie sheet. Mix sauce, desired meat, and cheese. Spoon into biscuits. Add onions, peppers, and seasoning as desired. Follow biscuit directions for baking. Enjoy!

Pizzas in a Blanket

    canned biscuit dough
    pizza or tomato sauce
    cheese
    meat (cooked)

Lay biscuits on a cookie sheet and press them out a little bit. Add mixture of sauce and meats and seasonings to each biscuit. (Allow a fairly large spoonful of mixture.) Fold biscuits around mixture and press on the ends. Follow biscuit directions for baking.

The Chicken Ran Off with the Stuffing Dish

    stuffing mix
    chicken pieces (raw)
    1 can cream of mushroom soup
    ⅓ c. milk
    1 pat butter or margarine

Mix and heat 4 cups of stuffing mix, 1¼ cups boiling water, butter or margarine. Place mixture into a casserole dish. Cook chicken pieces about 5 minutes in the microwave, then place around edges of casserole. Mix cream of mushroom soup and milk then pour over chicken and stuffing. Bake at 400° for 30 minutes or until chicken is done.

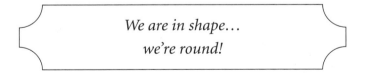

We are in shape…
we're round!

Mashed Potato Stuffers

    mashed potatoes (leftovers or fresh)
    shredded cheese
    onion powder

large pasta shells
onions
peppers
seasonings

Prepare pasta shells per package instructions. Drain and place in large casserole dish. Mix mashed potatoes, shredded cheese and onion powder. Stuff mixture into cooked pasta shells. Add cooked onions, peppers, or seasonings as desired. Pour over shells. Bake in the oven (300°) or cook in the microwave until cheese is melted and potatoes are warm. Some people like to broil this casserole until all is melted—but watch carefully so it doesn't burn. Serve with sour cream.

Mama's Money-Saving Meatloaf

Loaf
1 lb. ground beef (include any leftover hamburger
 you have)
1 cup of bread crumbs or small pieces
 of regular bread
1 c. milk
1 egg
Worcestershire sauce
salt and pepper
onions, peppers, mushrooms

Topping
⅔ c. ketchup
¼ c. mustard (regular or spice)
1 T. brown sugar

Mix loaf ingredients and form in loaf pan. Mix topping ingredients together and spread on top of meat loaf. Cook for 45 minutes at 350°.

Hint: Leftover slices of meatloaf make wonderful lunchtime sandwiches.

Crockpot Medley

1 can corn soup
½ c. milk
2 c. of broccoli flowerets
1 c. sliced or canned carrots
1 c. cauliflowerets
½ c. shredded cheese

Put all ingredients except cheese in a crockpot and cook on low for approximately 4 hours. Add shredded cheese 10 or 15 minutes before serving.

> *Don't underestimate the "dinner when you get home" appliance—the crockpot.*

Cheap Chili

2 cans chili-style chunky tomatoes
1 can kernel corn (drained)
1 can rinsed and drained chili beans

Combine and serve over hot dogs.

Tortilla Chili Bowl

tortilla chips
chili (canned or fresh)
shredded cheese

Layer tortilla chips on the bottom and sides of a large bowl. Pour chili on top of the chips. Sprinkle shredded cheese on top and microwave until hot. Serve with tossed salad.

Quick Chicken Cutlets

> breaded chicken cutlets (frozen)
> ham, turkey, or chicken (leftovers work great!)
> Swiss or American cheese

Add slices of Swiss or American cheese and leftover ham or turkey to the top of frozen breaded chicken cutlets and heat until the cheese is melted. Add a baked potato and vegetable and you have your meal.

Sassy Sauces for Chicken:

> • fresh tomatoes (chopped) and salsa
> • apricot jam, spiced mustard, cider vinegar
> • melted butter and hot sauce (great for buffalo wings)

Raving Ramen Recipes

Ramen or other "just add water" noodles are about the cheapest noodles you can buy. Add any vegetables (can be frozen) you desire and cook. If you add leftover chicken, turkey, or ham you'll have a wonderful hot entree or cold pasta salad.

Potato Topper Supper

> baking potatoes
> chicken, ham, or turkey
> chili (prepared)
> chopped onions
> peppers
> mushrooms
> broccoli
> cauliflower
> sour cream

Bake potatoes as usual. Put leftover dices of chicken, ham, chili, or turkey in separate bowls. Also have chopped onions, peppers, mushrooms, sour cream, broccoli, and cauliflower in separate bowls. Have everyone create his or her own favorite combination. Great for buffet-style serving or barbecues! Serve with salad.

Spaghetti Sense

spaghetti
creamed spinach (frozen)
Parmesan cheese
french bread

Cook spaghetti and creamed spinach. Combine. Add Parmesan cheese and serve over bread. Toss a salad and you have a quick meal.

Macaroni Meal

1 pkg. macaroni and cheese mix
ground beef
½ c. salsa

Prepare the macaroni and cheese mix per instructions. Add cooked ground beef and salsa. Put in a casserole dish and bake 20 minutes at 400°. Serve with a salad and bread.

Stewing Around

canned carrots, drained
2 potatoes (canned if desired)
2 small onions
1 pkg. frozen peas
1 pkg. wieners, sliced
1 can cream of celery soup
1 jar processed cheese spread

Cook potatoes and chop up. Then combine all ingredients. Heat and serve. This also works great using a crockpot!

Spam to the Rescue

1 can Spam
1 large can sliced pineapples
brown sugar
dry mustard mix

Put four thickly sliced Spam into a casserole dish "standing up." Drain the pineapple and set juice aside. Place pineapple slices between each slice of Spam. Add rest of drained pineapple slices around the edges of casserole dish. Bake at 350° for 25 minutes. You may need to baste occasionally.

Tuna Veggie Burgers

2 cans drained tuna
2 c. bread crumbs
1 egg
chopped onions

Mix all ingredients together in a large bowl. Form into patties on a greased cookie sheet and bake for 15 minutes at 350°.

> *Always serve large portions of fill-up foods such as potatoes, pasta, and rice.*

Peanut Butter Sandwich Surprise

½ c. peanut butter
shredded cheese
shredded carrots
¼ c. orange marmalade

Mix ingredients in a large bowl. Spread on raisin bread (or any bread of your choice) and serve.

Hint: This mixture made ahead of time and kept in the refrigerator is great for those rushed morning breakfasts and after-school snacks. Yes, these may *sound* yucky—but they are delicious!

Pan of Chicken Pot Pie

    2 cans cream of broccoli soup
    1 c. milk
    pepper as desired
    4 c. of cut-up vegetables (cauliflower, carrots,
      broccoli—or leftovers!)
    1 can biscuit dough
    2 c. cubed, cooked chicken, turkey, or other leftover meat

Mix everything together, then bake at 400° for 15 minutes or until it bubbles. Remove from oven and stir mixture. Arrange biscuits over mixture and bake an additional 15 minutes or until biscuits are golden brown.

Chicken Delight

    chicken, cut up
    1 envelope of onion soup mix
    2 T. water
    1 T. oil

Place chicken in casserole dish. Combine other ingredients, then pour over chicken. Bake 45 minutes at 375°.

Note: Need a creative side dish for chicken? Stir fry in butter leftover coleslaw and serve.

Give-Me-a-Break Casserole

    1 lb. sausage or ham
    6 slices of bread
    8 eggs
    ½ c. margarine
    chopped peppers
    chopped onions
    2½ c. milk
    salt and pepper
    shredded cheese

Place bread in a casserole dish. Mix together: eggs, margarine, chopped peppers, chopped onions, milk, salt, pepper, and meat. Pour over the bread. Bake at 350° for 45 to 50 minutes. Add shredded cheese just before end of cooking time, if desired. Refrigerate overnight. Heat and serve.

This casserole is wonderful and keeps in the refrigerator for approximately 5 days. Perfect for those morning rushes or to take to work with you!

Our Favorite "Throw Together" Recipe

    2 lb. bag Tater Tots
    2 cans cream of mushroom soup
    2 lb. bag frozen vegetables (can also use fresh)
    Cheetos or other cheese crunch snack food

Throw in a large baking dish Tater Tots, mushroom soup, and vegetables. Add 2 to 3 tablespoons of water. Bake until potatoes are done. Top with cheese and Cheetos for pizzazz.

Breakfast Wraps

Have you ever had one of those delicious breakfast wraps? Make them yourself using leftovers!

soft tortillas
eggs
bacon or sausage
chopped onions or peppers

Take a soft tortilla and fill it with leftover eggs, bacon or sausage, chopped onions or peppers. Wrap it up like a burrito and enjoy!

Make up several and have them ready to grab on your way out to work. These wraps are good anytime. Use leftover chicken or turkey and your leftover salad when you need a change of pace for lunches and suppers.

> *Put a lid on your food spending for lunches, suppers, and the food you take to work! Keep your leftover food in single-serving containers ready to use. You can also freeze them so you can use them when you're in a rush.*

Bread
Beautiful Baking Bread

Makes 2 loaves.

1 T. orange rind
¾ c. orange juice
¼ c. butter
1 c. sugar
1 egg
fruit (cranberries, dried fruit, etc.)
2 c. all-purpose flour
1½ tsp. baking soda

pinch of salt
1 cup walnuts (or other nuts)

Preheat oven to 325° and oil your loaf pans.

Add orange rind to orange juice. Cream together butter, sugar, and egg. Add desired fruit.

Sift together flour, baking soda, and salt. Add nuts (optional).

Blend dry mix with orange juice mixture. The batter will be pretty stiff.

Divide batter and place in 2 loaf pans. Bake for 1¼ hours. Test with toothpick. (Poke toothpick into bread. If it comes out clean the bread is done!) Remove loaves from pans and cool.

These loaves are perfect for holidays or giving to someone going through difficulties. Wrap in cellophane plastic (that comes in colors) or use plain clear wrap and do your own decorating.

Knead Bread

1 T. active dry yeast
1 T. sugar
5 ½ c. flour

Add active dry yeast to water that is the temperature and feeling of bath water. Then add sugar and wisk until sugar is dissolved. Add flour *slowly,* continually whisking.

Start kneading dough by turning over in half and then pressing down with your palm. Keep doing this for 10 minutes. Set aside for 1 or 2 hours in a bowl and cover with plastic wrap. The dough will double in size.

"Punch down" or flatten dough. Knead it again, shape it and place in a loaf pan. Cook for approximately 1 hour at 350°.

Crescent Rolls

8 oz. can crescent biscuit dough (cheapest you can find)
⅓ cup chopped cranberries

2 T. cracker crumbs
1 tsp. grated orange peel
pinch of sugar

Unroll the dough and divide into 8 triangles. Add all other ingredients by spreading them onto each triangle. Roll them up, and bake as directed on biscuit dough package. Wonderful for snacks, company, parties, and reunions.

Onion Crescents

8 oz. can crescent biscuit dough
½ T. butter
1 tsp. minced onion
1 tsp. parsley flakes, dried

Prepare canned crescent rolls as directed on package. Place on a cookie sheet. Mix together melted butter, minced onion, and parsley. (Add more butter if necessary to stick the toppings on the rolls.) Brush on dough and bake as directed. These are good served by themselves or with any kind of dip. (Spinach dip is especially tasty.)

Country Crescents

8 oz. can crescent biscuit dough
1 T. sour cream
½ tsp. minced onions
½ tsp. parsley flakes, dried
½ tsp. ground sage
¼ tsp. celery salt

Divide crescent dough into 8 triangles. Mix together sour cream, minced onion, parsley flakes, ground sage, and celery salt. Spread over each triangle and roll as usual. Bake per biscuit dough package instructions. Delicious, delicious, delicious!

Hint: Use your imagination when preparing crescent rolls. Ingredients you can add include: shredded cheese, dried fruit, and chopped onions.

Gingerbread Bread

2½ c. whole-wheat flour
1¼ c. molasses
1 tsp. baking soda
½ c. oil
1 tsp. ginger
½ c. boiling water
pinch of salt
pinch of cinnamon
¼ cup raisins

Mix together the flour, baking soda, ginger, salt, and cinnamon. Then, in a separate bowl, mix together the molasses, oil, water, and raisins. Combine all ingredients and stir until smooth. Pour into greased 9-inch square pan. Bake at 350° for 55 minutes. To test doneness lightly push down on bread. It will spring back when done. Let cool and cut in squares to serve. (Freezes well.)

Peter-Peter Pumpkin Bread

1 c. brown sugar
½ c. oil
2 eggs
1 c. canned pumpkin
1½ c. flour
1 tsp. baking soda
pinch of salt
1 tsp. baking powder
1½ tsp. cinnamon

½ tsp. cloves
½ tsp. ginger
creamy cream cheese

Mix in a large bowl the brown sugar, oil, eggs, and canned pumpkin. Beat until light. Stir in flour, baking soda, salt, and baking powder. Add cinnamon, cloves, and ginger.

Mix it. Mix it. And mix it well. Pour into a greased 9 x 5-inch loaf pan. Bake at 350° for 45 minutes.

Do the toothpick test in the center. (Poke with toothpick. If toothpick comes out clean, the bread is done.) Cool for 15 minutes *after* you have eased it out of the pan. Makes about 18 slices. Serve with creamy cream cheese—delicious!

What wonderful bread to wrap decoratively for gifts. Have fun by adding holiday decorations. This bread also freezes well.

Beverages

Breakfast Drinks on the Run

Here are eight ideas to add to skim or low-fat milk for a quick morning drink or an afternoon health drink.

- Add splashes of vanilla, almond, maple, or rum extract
- 1 tsp. fat free hot fudge and ¼ c. mineral or distilled water
- ½ c. pureed strawberries (frozen is cheaper, but you can use fresh)
- 2 tsp. orange juice concentrate (or regular canned orange juice) and ½ tsp. vanilla
- 2 tsp. instant malted milk powder
- ½ c. root beer and a tiny scoop of low- or no-fat ice cream or ice milk
- Blended banana with 1 tsp. honey and ¼ tsp. vanilla
- 2 tsp. fruit-flavored syrup

Hint: Why not make these drinks ahead of time? Your favorite drink mixture can be kept in a pitcher or single-serve drink containers in the refrigerator. Then you can easily enjoy it at home or on the way to work. If you keep these nutritious drinks ready-to-pour, your kids will love them and get their calcium as well.

Here's a Pumpkin Hint!

When you purchase pumpkins each year in the Fall it's more than a decoration! When your pumpkin is about ready to get mushy, place it somewhere in your yard and leave it. It will go to seed, and you'll have pumpkins next year. (It doesn't hurt to rake the soil and press the seeds into it a bit.) Pumpkins can bring in quite a bit of money if you sell them in your front yard during the Fall season. Do it on weekends and you'll be surprised at how many people stop and buy!

Sum/Sum/Summer Cooler

2 c. skim milk
2 c. unsweetened pineapple juice
1 tsp. vanilla
1 tsp. coconut extract
2 T. sugar

Mix all ingredients together and pour into cold, iced-filled glasses. Add little umbrellas and imagine you are somewhere in the tropics on a warm beach. This will help you survive the summer—and you won't be such a crab when August temperatures have you wilting in the sun!

Monkey Breakfast Shake

1½ c. skim milk
1 peeled banana, medium (*Hint:* freeze the banana in plastic overnight)
½ tsp. vanilla
cinnamon (optional)

Blend all ingredients in a blender and pour—a delightful, healthy, good mornin' pick-me-up.

Option: Sprinkle some cinnamon on top before serving to add a little zest.

Ring Around the Punch Bowl

Perk up your punch and punch bowl. Freeze water and fruit together in a ring-shaped mold (perhaps a gelatin mold) and put it into the punch bowl. This looks pretty, keeps punch cold, and gradually you'll get to enjoy the fruit!

Perfect Lemonade

Did you know that if you mix ½ c. of lemon juice and ½ c. sugar to a quart of water, you are making the best and cheapest lemonade you can find! You can also freeze this lemonade in popsicle molds. A cool, inexpensive treat for the kids!

Pink Pigs

Use reconstituted powdered or regular milk and add cranberry juice.

Purple People Eaters

Add grape juice to reconstituted powdered or regular milk so your children can become purple-people eaters.

Cran-Punch

1 gal. cranberry juice (or other flavor)
½ c. sugar
½ c. lemon juice
1 c. orange juice
1 quart seltzer or light-colored soft drink

Mix juice or punch drink (cranberry juice, cran-grape, or any cran-juice you desire) with sugar, lemon juice, and orange juice. Keep in the refrigerator. When you are ready to serve the punch, add ice and the seltzer or soft drink.

Note: For a touch of class, add scoops of sherbet or ice cream instead of ice. The punch will eventually become creamy and delicious.

Coffee Treat

¼ c. instant coffee
3 c. chocolate or mocha flavoring

whipped cream
chocolate sprinkles
cinnamon

Heat 2 cups of water and let simmer. Add instant coffee and chocolate or flavoring. Pour into individual cups and top with whipped cream. Add chocolate sprinkles or cinnamon if desired.

Note: Mixture can also be refrigerated and served cold.

Hawaiian Punch

¼ quart nonfat dry milk or regular milk
1 c. punch drink (any flavor)
½ tsp. vanilla
12 oz. club soda
sherbet or no-fat ice cream.

In a pitcher, stir in milk, punch drink, vanilla, and club soda. Pour in glasses and top with ice cream.

Frosty Coffee

1½ c. cold, strong coffee
2 tsp. sugar
1 banana
½ pint frozen yogurt or ice cream

Cut banana into slices. In a blender, mix coffee, sugar, and the banana. Add frozen yogurt or ice cream (put blender on low after adding ice cream).

Cherry Dairy Sodas

1½ c. milk
10 oz. package strawberries

1 scoop strawberry ice cream
Black Cherry soda

Mix milk and strawberries in a blender. Pour into glasses and add a scoop of strawberry ice cream. Add black cherry soft drink to each glass.

Thirst Quickie Quencher

orange peels
orange juice

Place an orange peel in each ice cube section of an ice cube tray and fill each ice cube section with juice. Twist peel for decorative look. Freeze. When ready to serve pour rest of juice into glasses and add the orange-peel ice cubes.

Note: You can be really imaginative with this idea. Instead of orange peels, you might use coconut or lime peels. Try other juice flavors, too.

Frosty Rose

1 pt. strawberry ice cream
1 c. strawberries (frozen or fresh)
1 c. nonalcoholic rosé wine or ginger ale
½ c. milk

In a blender (on high), mix ice cream, strawberries, wine, and milk.

Easy Eggnog

12 large eggs
1¼ c. sugar
pinch of salt
1 qt. milk

This eggnog needs to be made 5 hours before you are going to serve it or the night before.

Beat eggs, sugar, and salt together with a whisk. Pour into saucepan. Slowly stir in milk. Heat on stove at low temperature. Stir constantly until the mixture thickens and will coat the back of a spoon. This should take about 30 minutes. Be careful: If this mixture boils, it will curdle and be ruined.

Snacks
Popcorn Concoction

  14 c. popped popcorn
  2 c. sugar
  1 c. light corn syrup
  ½ c. butter

Make a popcorn glaze by heating sugar, light corn syrup, water, and butter. Cook this until it hits hardball (250° to 268°). Stir glaze and popcorn together and start pressing them into balls or press them into large cookie cutters. To avoid burning your hands while forming balls, continually and liberally "butter" them. Also, be sure to grease your cookie cutters. Wrap popcorn balls in plastic and tie with ribbons. Perfect gifts for any occasion, especially Christmas.

Cheesy Tastin' Popcorn

  popcorn
  ¼ to ½ c. margarine
  ½ c. shredded cheddar cheese
  pinch of salt

Pop regular popcorn or microwave popcorn as usual. Mix together margarine, shredded cheddar cheese, and salt. Melt this mixture in the microwave or on the stove, then pour over popcorn. Mouth poppin' good!

Hint: Popcorn makes a great gift, especially if presented in cute canisters with ribbons and recipes attached.

Sweet Sleds

graham crackers
hard, round candy
candy canes
frosting (thick)

Use graham crackers as the sled platforms and add hard, round candies for seat backs and decoration. Candy canes make great sled blades. Glue all of this together with frosting. For unique sleds be creative with your candy choices.

Flying Lifesavers

Hot glue two sticks of gum (for wings) on a roll of lifesaver candy; one at the top and one on the bottom parallel to the top stick of gum for a biplane look. Glue a plastic wrapped hard candy on one of the ends for the propeller. You now have an edible lifesaving airplane!

Cheesy Sticks

Butter or margarine
Sourdough bread
Shredded cheese

Spread butter on slices of sourdough bread and sprinkle shredded cheese on top. Chill overnight covered. Cut the slices into 1-inch strips and cook in a toaster oven or broiler until they are brown. This will take approximately 10 minutes, so make sure your cheese doesn't burn. It's a yummy, cheesy thing.

Moldy Cheese

> 2 pkg. 8-oz. cream cheese
> ¾ c. to 1 c. salsa
> Tortilla chips or crackers

Stir and soften cream cheese. In a plastic-lined mold, pour in half of the cheese. Put the salsa over the cheese in the mold. Pour the rest of the cream cheese on top of the salsa. Refrigerate until firm, take out of mold, and present it on any of your favorite serving plates or dishes. Serve with tortilla chips or crackers.

Note: Your mold can be anything you have—a gelatin mold or a round or square bowl.

Wagon Wheels

> 2 pkg. 8-oz. cream cheese (softened)
> 1 pkg. Ranch salad dressing mix
> 2 or 3 green onions, diced
> 1 jar pimentos, drained
> 1 can sliced black olives, drained (optional)

Mix together ingredients then spread onto flour tortillas. Roll the tortillas firmly and tightly. Chill in refrigerator for 2 hours or more. Cut into wheels (rolls) and serve. They'll keep rolling, rolling, rolling...

Oyster Snacker Crackers

> 1 pkg. Ranch salad dressing mix
> ¾ c. oil
> 5 c. plain oyster crackers

Stir together ranch salad dressing mix and oil. Add oyster crackers. Place in the oven for 20 minutes at 250°. Stir the mixture occasionally.

Little Hams

8 oz can crescent roll dough
4 ham slices, thin
mustard
cheese

Unroll the crescent dough rolls into 4 long rectangles. Firmly seal or pinch together each piece to form solid rectangles. Place a slice of ham a little below center. Add mustard and cheese if desired. Roll up each rectangle, starting with the shortest end, and press the edges together. Slice each of the rolls into desired size. Place each slice, cut side down, onto a slightly greased cookie sheet. Bake 15 to 20 minutes at 375°.

Sausage Snacks

smoked sausage links (small)
crescent roll dough

Roll up a fully cooked smoked sausage link in each dough triangle. Bake at 375° for 15 minutes or until brown. These can be made ahead and refrigerated.

Easy Veggie Pizza

2 8-oz. cans crescent roll dough
veggies
sour cream
horseradish
salt and pepper

Separate crescent rolls and form into 4 long rectangles cross-wise on an ungreased baking pan. Press together the bottom and about 1 inch of each side. Bake at 375° for 15 to 20 minutes or until golden brown. When cooled, add to each crust: sour cream, horseradish, salt, and pepper. Also add desired veggies, such as broccoli flowerets, green peppers, green diced onions, sliced mushrooms, and chopped seedless tomatoes. Cut into small pieces and refrigerate before serving.

Party Bird Centerpiece

icing
pretzel sticks
crackers

Using thick icing, glue pretzel sticks (logs) together to construct a tiny bird house. Crackers (any kind) are great for roof shingles.

Note: Icing can be homemade or use marshmallow cream or cream cheese. Have some of the icing drip off the roof for a snow-fall effect. Only bird brains like ours could come up with this one! Wonderful to use as a centerpiece or as a happy gift to a bird watcher.

Baby Bagel Chips

bagels
garlic powder
Parmesan cheese
salt

Bagels getting hard? Slice bagels into thin circles and brush with a little oil. Sprinkle on garlic powder, Parmesan cheese, and salt. Heat in the microwave for two minutes (time varies depending on how many are cooking). If your microwave doesn't have a turntable, turn the slices once. What a healthy snack to take to work or school. Make a bunch at one time!

Sassy Salsa Dip

1-oz. pkg. dry party dip mix
1 pt. sour cream
½ c. chunky salsa

Mix party dip with sour cream then add chunky salsa. The easiest salsa dip around!

Saucepan Cheese Sauce Dip

butter
flour
milk
salt and pepper
shredded cheddar cheese

Melt butter, then stir in flour and milk. Add salt and pepper to taste. Cook on low heat until the sauce thickens. Add shredded cheddar cheese. Stir gently and continue cooking slowly until there are no lumps. Serve over rice, pasta, or meat. It's also great for adding zest to leftovers!

Easy Cheesy Ball

2 oz. softened cream cheese
1 tsp. minced onion
2 tsp. chopped or drained pimento
dash of garlic salt
2 T. mayonnaise or salad dressing
½ c. chopped green or red pepper
½ c. chopped walnuts
8 oz. shredded cheddar cheese.

Roll all ingredients into a ball for a great party snack. You could also make miniature balls and serve with chunks of fruit. Provide toothpicks for creating mini-kabobs.

Peanut Buttery Milkballs

½ c. honey
½ c. peanut butter (creamy or chunky)
1 c. dry milk
coconut
regular or powdered sugar
nuts

Combine honey, peanut butter, and dry milk and form into balls. Roll balls in the coconut, powdered sugar, regular sugar, or nuts for a festive treat. Keeps well in the refrigerator for serving later.

Note: For a party place the plain balls into a huge bowl and let the guests decide their own topping.

Popsicle Heads

4 T. margarine
10-oz. pkg. of regular marshmallows or 4 cups
   mini-marshmallows
food coloring
crunchy rice cereal
paper cups
Popsicle sticks
candy pieces

Melt margarine and add marshmallows and stir often until melted. Add 10 drops of food coloring, then pour over 6 cups of rice cereal. Mix well. Spoon and press into paper cups. Insert a popsicle stick into each cup. Let them set for approximately 30 minutes. Carefully tip off the cup. Press candy pieces into "heads" to make faces.

Desserts
Snowy Cones

1 envelope sweetened drink mix
½ c. cold water

Place sweetened drink mix in a bowl and add water. Stir until dissolved. Pour over glasses of crushed ice.

Butterfly Heart

Two heart-shaped molds or two heart-shaped cookie cutters placed together at the bottom point of each heart make a wonderful butterfly for you to decorate with candy for birthdays or other festive events.

Peppermint Mugs

hot cocoa or chocolate
peppermint ice cream
whipped cream
peppermint sticks

Fill mugs three-fourths full with hot cocoa. Add one scoop of peppermint ice cream. Top with a little whipped cream. Place peppermint sticks into cups for stirring.

Universal Icing

1 c. powdered sugar
1 egg-white
food coloring

With an electric mixer, mix powdered sugar, egg white, and food coloring. (This icing will harden and makes an excellent "glue" for gingerbread houses.)

Cheap Cheesecake

8-oz pkg. cream cheese
⅓ c. sugar
8-oz. tub whipped topping
graham-cracker pie crust
fruit

Mix softened cream cheese and sugar. Slowly stir in whipped topping. Spoon into graham-cracker pie crust. Refrigerate overnight (3 hours minimum), then top with cherries, strawberries, or blueberries before serving.

Fruit Pie

8-oz. pkg. gelatin (any flavor)
8 oz. whipped topping
fruit
1 graham-cracker pie crust

Dissolve gelatin package in boiling water as directed. Add 2 cups of ice cubes and stir for 3 minutes or until ice is melted. Stir in whipped topping and add desired fruit (strawberries, peaches, raspberries, blueberries). Place all ingredients into a graham-cracker crust. Chill for at least two hours before serving.

Fruity Baskets

A watermelon

Take a long watermelon and trim one end so it will stand on its own. Then, leaving a 1-inch wall in the center cut watermelon lengthwise on both sides stopping 5 inches from bottom. Carve out the watermelon "handle" and "basket" so you can fill it with fruit.

This works great with a cantaloupe too. Fill with any fruit desired mixed with the cut-up watermelon or cantaloupe.

Note: A zig-zag cutting tool or knife will help you scallop your melon basket edging.

Buggy Fruit

licorice sticks
dried fruit
icing

Kids love dried fruit bugs! Attach twizzler or short, sliced licorice stick candy "legs" all around two sides of dried fruit with small bits of icing "glue." Leave one end open for the head, but add a long licorice in the back for the tail.

Candy Cones

Fill empty ice cream cones with candy. Decorate the outside with icing and candy as desired.

Peanut Buttery Topping

2 T. peanut butter
1 T. maple syrup

Over medium heat, stir peanut butter and maple syrup until it is smooth. Pour it over ice cream. Yummy and easy...

Birthday Wishes

Write "Happy Birthday" around the sides of your dessert plates with a gel or regular icing tube. Use this idea for any holiday or special occasion.

Sticky Popsicles

2 c. sugar
⅔ c. light corn syrup
1 tsp. vanilla
food coloring
ribbons or Popsicle sticks

Over low heat, stir together sugar, corn syrup, and ½ cup water until dissolved. Bring this to a boil by increasing heat. Without stirring, cook for an additional 15 to 20 minutes. Temperature should reach 300° on a candy thermometer. Remove from heat, then add your favorite food coloring color and vanilla. Pour this mixture into various shapes on a foil lined baking sheet. Be creative on the shaping. Press ribbons or Popsicle sticks horizontally into each one for handles. Decorate with sprinkles. Cool at room temperature before serving.

Jelly Belly Cookies

1½ c. butter
1 c. sugar
4 egg yolks (large)
4 c. flour
jelly

Beat together softened butter and sugar until fluffy. Add egg yolks and beat thoroughly. Gradually add in flour and blend well until you have a firm batter. Pull off small sections (2 tsp. each) and roll into balls. Place these 2 inches apart on an ungreased baking sheet. Using the back of a spoon, make a single impression or dent in each cookie. Bake at 325° for 10 minutes. Remove from oven and spoon your favorite jelly into the center of each cookie. Bake 15 minutes or until cookies are light brown. Cool and eat.

Note: This recipe makes 10 dozen cookies! Perfect for a crowd.

Heavenly Angel Cakes

- Cut a whole angel food cake in half crosswise. Remove the top, then spread whipped cream and sliced berries of your choice on top of bottom piece. Replace the top and crown with more cream and berries.
- Toast slices of angel food cake and add ice cream and toppings of your choice.
- Serve each angel food cake slice in a pool of fruit puree or tasty dessert sauce. Add fresh fruit around the side of each plate.
- Tear angel food cake into pieces and make your first layer in a large bowl. Cover with pudding and/or sliced fruit. Repeat the steps of layering. Top with whipped cream and serve.
- Make small holes in an angel food cake, then cover cake with your favorite dessert topping. Add fruit on top of the cake or on the sides. Top with whipped cream.

Birthday Candle Dilemma

Why are you buying so many candles to top that birthday cake for someone who may require 2 packages of candles? Instead use candy to outline the age of the birthday guest on top of the cake. Add *one* candle in the middle to keep the fun of blowing out a candle.

Cheesy Brownies

> 3 oz. unsweetened chocolate (chopped or chips)
> ½ tsp. salt
> ¾ c. no- or low-fat cottage cheese
> ½ c. powdered sugar
> candy sprinkles

Melt unsweetened chocolate on low and let it cool for 5 minutes. Puree salt, cottage cheese, and powdered sugar until smooth. Add chocolate and mix together. Pour mixture into lightly greased 8-inch square baking pan. Bake for 20 minutes or until it sets. Sprinkle with more powdered sugar or sprinkles. Cut into squares, and invite 16 people over to have one brownie each...or 4 people to have 4 brownies each!

Orangey Pumpkins

> oranges
> ice cream
> chocolate cookies
> nuts
> whipped cream

Cut the top off of an orange. Scrape out the insides, like you would a miniature pumpkin. Carve eyes, nose, and mouth—again, as you would a pumpkin. Spoon some ice cream into the orange. Add a layer of chocolate cookies. Top this with nuts and a small amount of whipped cream. Replace the top and wrap with plastic. Freeze until serving time.

Pokey Cake

> cake
> gelatin
> food coloring

Bake a cake as usual. Poke holes in the top with an ice pick or skewers and pour dissolved gelatin into the holes. Use any colors you want to, for instance red and green would be fantastic colors for Christmas.

Note: May also use instant pudding, but use the end of a wooden spoon to make larger holes.

Cake Salute

    cake
    nondairy whipped topping
    blueberries
    strawberries

Make a rectangular-shaped cake as usual and top it with non-dairy whipped topping. Create a flag design by arranging stars (blueberries) in the top left corner and stripes (strawberries that are cut in half lengthwise). Refrigerate until you're ready to serve. You will be the talk of the Fourth of July picnic with this one!

Patriotic Dessert

    1 cake
    2 4-oz. pkgs. of blue colored gelatin
    2 4-oz. pkgs. of red colored gelatin
    whipped topping
    strawberries
    blueberries
    sprinkles

Bake a rectangular-shaped cake. Cut into bite-sized squares. Prepare blue gelatin and red gelatin. *Cook the different colors of gelatin separately!* Pour gelatin into separate 13 x 9-inch pans for 3 hours then cut into ½-inch cubes. (Gelatin must be firm before cutting.) Layer gelatin cubes, whipped topping, cut up cake, and strawberries into a large serving bowl. Garnish with some of the gelatin cubes, sprinkles, strawberries or blueberries.

Mini Cakes

½ c. sugar
8-oz. pkg. softened cream cheese
½ c. milk
3½ c. whipped topping
sponge cake shells (often used for strawberry shortcake)
sliced fruit

Mix sugar and softened cream cheese together. Gradually beat in milk until smooth. Stir in whipped topping. Mix well. Spoon ⅓ c. of the mixture into sponge cake shells. Add sliced fruit to make faces for the children or flowers for the adults. Let your imagination go!

Cloudy Dessert

3-oz. pkg. gelatin (any flavor)
whipped topping (nondairy)

Make gelatin as usual. Pour into 8-inch square pan and chill until firm (approximately 3 hours). Cut into cubes. (Dip knife into hot water to make it easier to slice the gelatin.) Spoon nondairy whipped topping into the bottom of dessert dishes, making a small indent in the middle and pushing some of the whipped topping up on the sides of the dessert dishes to create a pillow/cloud effect. Spoon the gelatin cubes into the center. Keep chilled until serving. Top with more whipped topping if desired.

Note: This also works with pudding instead of whipped topping.

Coffee Can Ice Cream

1 c. milk
1 c. whipping cream
½ c. sugar
½ tsp. vanilla
nuts (optional)
fruit (optional)
rock salt
1 lb. coffee can
3 lb. coffee can

Put all of the food ingredients (not the rock salt) in a clean 1-lb. coffee can. Put lid on, then place into the larger coffee can. Pack crushed ice *between* the cans. Pour ¾ cup of rock salt evenly over the crushed ice. Put the lid on. Roll can back and forth on a table for about 10 minutes or let the kids carefully roll it back and forth on the floor). Take out the smaller can, open the lid, and stir the mixture. Place in cones or cups and enjoy!

Peanut Butter Cookies

Easiest snack ever!

1 c. peanut butter (low-fat okay)
1 c. sugar
1 c. flour

Mix ingredients together and roll into balls or flatten and cut. Voila!—peanut butter cookies!

Yummy Dirt Pudding

2 3.4-oz. pkgs. chocolate pudding (makes 8 servings)
3½ c. milk
3 c. whipped topping
16 oz. pkg. cookies (crushed)

Make chocolate pudding as directed except use 3½ cups of milk. Let cool for 5 minutes, then stir in 3 cups of whipped topping and half of the cookies. Spoon into a 13 x 9-inch dish and sprinkle on the remaining cookie crumbs. Refrigerate for an hour before serving. Decorate with Gummy Worms for more fun.

Cubby Print Cupcakes

cupcakes
white frosting
Junior Mints
Hershey's Kisses

Bake your favorite cupcake recipe, and top each cake with white icing. Place one junior mint on top in the middle, and place three chocolate Kisses (points up) around the mint to form a paw print.

Cool, Cold Sandwiches

Makes 12 sandwiches

½ c. corn syrup
½ c. peanut butter
4 c. crispy rice cereal
ice cream

Stir corn syrup and peanut butter together. Add crispy rice cereal and stir until well blended. Press mixture evenly in a lightly buttered 13 x 9-inch pan and place in freezer or coldest part of refrigerator until firm. Cut cereal mixture into 12 3-inch squares. Make sandwiches by placing ice cream (cut into slices) between two squares. Individually wrap and place in freezer.

Kitchen Tips and Grocery Hints

- Add granola or any crunchy cereal to cookies and brownies for a delicious snack.

- Put flour in an unused salt shaker and keep it in the freezer. Use it when you have to lightly flour a pan.

- Store ice cream and Popsicles in a plastic container so they don't drip or get stuck in your freezer. Leave the top off.

- For wonderful frosting, add maple syrup to confectioner's sugar and stir until thick.

- Mix the more expensive, brand-name sugary cereals with a large box of generic cereal.

- Do your weekly grocery shopping after you've cleaned your house and finished the laundry so you can concentrate on getting bargains.

- Label your refrigerator shelves: leftovers, fruit, drinks, and condiments. This makes filling out your grocery list so much easier and saves you time and money in not buying what you already have.

- Add chocolate syrup to regular oatmeal for a special treat.

- Spices don't have to be expensive, though the name brands often are. Go to your local bag-it-yourself grocery store; you will be amazed at the low price for spices on generic brands—and they are just as flavorful. Also check out the bulk-food section.

If at first you don't succeed,
try reading the recipe.

- Don't be intimidated by impatient grocery cashiers when they see you coming with your coupons. It's your money you're saving, not theirs!

- Every little bit helps—a $5 savings a week at the grocery store is a whopping $250 per year! Look for stores that double or triple coupons.

- Use jars and generic plastic containers. They keep leftovers just as well as those expensive name-brand containers.

- Revive yesterday's rolls by spraying them with cold water, putting them in a paper bag, and warming them in the microwave (or in the oven at 350° for 10 minutes).

- Comparison shopping between brand-name merchandise, generic, and store brands can lead to big savings.

- Buying things in bigger quantities does not always mean cheaper. Check the price per ounce!

- Reuse your plastic sandwich and plastic bags. Refill with the same type of food!

- Save cereal box liners to use as waxed paper when making pies and cookies.

- Leave a stick of celery in the bread bag to keep it fresh.

- Make your own flavored coffee by adding cocoa, cinnamon, and vanilla flavoring to your regular ground coffee. Brew as usual.

- To make your own flavored tea, add lemonade, orange juice, or a cheap punch mixture.

- Milk will last longer if you add a pinch of salt to it.

The Joys of Dieting

The Non-Stress Diet

This diet is designed to help you cope with the kind of stress that often accumulates during a typical day.

Breakfast

l grapefruit
1 slice whole wheat toast, dry
8 oz. skim milk

Lunch

4 oz. lean, broiled chicken breast
l c. steamed spinach
l c. herb tea
l Oreo cookie

Midafternoon Snack

rest of the Oreos in the package
2 pts. Rocky Road ice cream
l jar hot fudge sauce
nuts, cherries, whipped cream

Dinner

2 loaves garlic bread with cheese
large sausage, mushroom, and cheese pizza
3 Milky Way or Snickers candy bars

Diet Rules

1. If you eat something and no one else sees you, it has no calories.

2. When drinking a diet soda while eating a candy bar, the calories in the candy bar are canceled by the diet soda.

3. When you eat with someone else, calories don't count as long as you don't eat more than your friend.

4. Foods used for medicinal purposes never count. Example: hot chocolate, toast, cheesecake.

5. If you fatten up everyone else around you, you'll look thinner.

6. Movie-related foods do not have calories because they are part of the entertainment package. This includes Milk Duds, buttered popcorn, Junior Mints, and Tootsie Rolls.

7. Cookie pieces have no calories. (The process of breaking the cookie causes calorie loss.)

8. Foods licked off knives and spoons have no calories.

9. Foods of the same color such as green salad and Key Lime pie have the same number of calories.

Daddy's Hands

Turning Trash into Treasures

As you can see by this wonderful photo of our Daddy, he was as comfortable wearing sawdust as our Mama was wearing her apron. Whenever we hear Wynonna Judd sing the country song "Daddy's Hands" on the radio, none of us can keep tears from slipping down our cheeks. Daddy was tough, but loving. A tight budget and four kids caused him to be the father of creative home furnishings.

We loved the sounds and smells of his workshop and often wandered in to check on his latest creation. His work truck, too, was a wonder to us. It was filled with tiny compartments with little doors on the side to hold his tools. (Daddy was a director of buildings and grounds for the public school system in our area.) The house we grew up in was a large, green, two-story frame with an expansive porch and four big bedrooms upstairs. To us it was a dream house, filled with pint-sized nooks and crannies for endless games of hide-n-go-seek or for sneaking away to read a book in silence. One year Daddy made an L-shaped couch frame (mama sewed the cushions) and a matching coffee table from scraps of wood. In the nook under the stairway, Daddy made a built-in dresser and used our old wooden toy blocks to create unique handles. When we were babies, Daddy made us twins a double highchair and stroller to help Mama corral us.

Daddy loved a bargain as much as our mother (which explains why we got a double-dose of cheapskate genes). One day, after World War II, he came home from the Army–Navy supply store with a surplus bolt of navy-blue fabric. By the time we had slept on navy-blue pillowcases, dressed our dolls in navy-blue ensembles, sat on navy-blue cushions, picnicked on navy-blue tablecloths, and wore an endless supply of navy-blue jumpers we never wanted to see a navy-blue anything again!

During holiday seasons, Daddy would get especially creative. He set up a nice glowing "fire" by screwing a red light bulb into some fake logs and plugging it in. We awoke on Christmas morning, at age six, to the sight of two small wooden doll cradles and little rocking chairs that "Santa" had made for us. (Is Christmas morning ever as thrilling as it is when we are six years old?) Today we delight in watching our grandchildren rocking their baby dolls and tucking them into bed in these hand-me-down heirlooms.

As you might imagine, Daddy's love for creating something unique out of things other people might throw away was a trait he passed down to us. Here are some of our favorite projects for furnishing and decorating your home and entertaining the kids on a shoestring budget. In addition, we've sprinkled in some fun holiday decorating tips in memory of that wonderful "roaring" light bulb in our holiday fireplace.

Bedrooms

- A chest of drawers with a foam pad secured on top and bumper pads nailed to the wood around the pad makes a nice baby-changing table.

- Need bunk beds and all you have are twin beds? Position one bed on top of the other and anchor securely with screws and bolts. If the legs are too tall, cut the legs from the top bed to fit. If you need to, securely fasten boards to top frame for longer legs.

- Use an old belt to store hair bows and barrettes. Just clip them on the long part of the belt, which has been hung by the buckle on a nail or over a coat hanger.

- Hang a six-pack ring on a hanger and loop scarves, belts, and ties through the holes. Instant organization!

- The toes of old, clean, pantyhose can be stuffed with potpourri or a scented cotton ball and placed in your dresser drawers.

- Save your kids' old trucks, wagons, and boats and use them as plant holders for their rooms or play yard. Or use them for unique pencil holders or catch-alls.

- When storing shoes, put them in old socks to protect them.

- An unused baby crib makes a great doll or teddy bear collection place until the crib is needed again or given away. It is also handy to store clothes fresh from the dryer (keeps them off the floor) until you have time to sort and fold.

- Top a long, low dresser with a foam pad for a great youth bed. Add a ladder for convenience and fun.

• If you have a house full of kids (that will soon turn into a house full of slumber-partying teenagers), never throw away the mattress to a sleeper sofa that has seen better days. The mattress will come in handy when guests come, and it can be stored under a regular bed.

Family Areas

• Don't forget to save that old compact mirror (taken out of the compact) to use as a reflective base for a votive candle. The effect is so beautiful that it can turn a hot dog dinner into an event! And the old compact sans mirror can be used for a pill box, safety pins, hairpins, small hooks, or a toothpick carrier.

• Pantyhose makes wonderful stuffing for pillows and stuffed animals.

• Interesting old pie plates can serve as beautiful burner covers. You can also paint them or decorate as you like.

• Bandannas come in all colors as do scarves. They are great for covering bar stools and seats of small chairs.

• Save foam packing and use it instead of floral foam for your flower arrangements.

• Wrap an old throw pillow in material, gathering the front with a rubber band, poof it, then put the loose ends under the rubber band for a rosette.

• Cut out the middle of a worn braided rug and use it as a smaller area rug.

• Old weatherboard or pieces of molding can become a hat or coat rack by adding nails or hooks.

- Roll wet newspapers together tightly, bind them with wire, and let them dry. You will have a nice fire log in approximately 20 to 30 days ready for burning in the fireplace.

- Ornaments that have broken hooks can be arranged in a glass bowl filled with water and floating candles for an elegant centerpiece

- Need some toy boxes? Use clothes hampers and decorated with stickers or run ribbons or material through the webbing.

- If you can braid hair, you can braid strips of fabric together to make rag rugs.

- Save old lunch boxes. They make great sewing kits, snack boxes, first aid containers, cassette holders—the list is endless!

- To make flower arrangements look extra special, use a unique container for the vase such as an old wine bottle, medicine bottle, or jar.

- Be creative with curtain tie backs. Use old belts, scarves, raffia, vines, old stringed beads, bandannas, lace, necklaces, and on and on and on!

- Gather sticks from the yard and paint them bright colors. Place them in a tall container for a unique arrangement. You can make this a seasonal "tree" by hanging Easter, Christmas, birthday, or Valentine decorations on it.

- Empty the insides of large old stereo speakers and use as decorative boxes or for storage.

- Outdoor twigs can be cut and nailed or glued onto containers to create rustic desk sets and organizers.

- Save the wooden handles of old brooms, mops, or rakes. They make great dowel rods. Use for curtains, closets, and organizing.

- Turn a slatted side of an old crib lengthwise to hold magazines or towels.

- Make a coffee table from an old window, door, or board. Use bricks or flower pots for legs.

- Six-pack plastic rings are wonderful drapery rings. Cut off all but two rings, nail to the window corner, and thread fabric through ring. Puff up fabric around the rings until rings are hidden and material forms attractive folds.

- For fun family floor pillows stuff the legs of old sweat pants and blue jeans then sew them up. These also make great pillows for a college dorm if you use T-shirts or sweats with the college insignia on them!

- An old board with two pieces of wide ribbon nailed horizontally at the top and bottom and hung on the wall makes a nice catch-all for notes, cards, and booklets.

- An old, used small table + paint and stenciling = adorable end table.

- Cover a coffee can with lace to make a nice vase.

- Paint bottle caps gold or silver and push into a Styrofoam® wreath for a unique creation. Add lace or a ribbon behind the caps if desired.

- Brighten an old frame or wreath by gluing on leaves and lightly spraying it with gold paint. Add a colorful ribbon for zest.

- Cover a brick with fabric and use as a door stop.

- Couch got the slumps? (This happens a lot with hide-a-bed couches.) Add a board underneath the cushions.

- Cover ugly stools or wooden fruit crates by stapling on fabric. Fabric is cheaper than new furniture.

- Stuff the legs of old sweat pants to use as a door draftcatcher.

- Pop can tabs and paper clips make great picture hangers.

- Pieces of broken china or glass can be glued onto a frame to create a unique mosaic. Or jazz up an old picture frame by gluing on buttons or small pebbles.

> ***Recycling Fact:*** *In the United States we throw away enough aluminum every three months to rebuild our entire commercial airfleet.*

Kitchen/Bath/Utility Room

- Line drawers with placemats that you are tired of or don't use anymore.

- Thread a cord through the casing end of a pillowcase to make a laundry bag.

- A plastic one-gallon milk jug with a hole cut in the middle of it is a great holder for almost 100 plastic bags.

- Need a step stool? Cut the legs off of an old kitchen stool.

- Nylon fishing line can replace your commode's flapper chain when it dies.

- An old chandelier, sans the light bulbs, makes a wonderful holder for kitchen pots and pans. Just get some hooks, paint it, and hang in the middle of your kitchen or above your stove.

- Don't throw out those cute International Coffee® tins. They are not only decorative, they are perfect for storing tiny kitchen items, spices, corn-cob holders, icing tube tips, cinnamon and sugar mixture for toast, or your own custom spice mix.

- An old dresser drawer handle can make a stunning towel holder for the kitchen.

- Before you throw away any garment, snip off all the buttons, elastic, zipper, or decorations and store in your sewing chest.

- Save the plastic bottoms of liter bottles. They make excellent waterproof containers for sponges and soaps for under the kitchen sink.

- Save the unused shower caps from hotels to cover bowls of leftovers in your refrigerator.

- Save those small bottles of shampoo and conditioner from motels. Refill them when they're empty and use them when traveling or use for lotion to carry in your purse.

> ***Recycling Fact:*** *Making one aluminum can instead of a glass bottle saves energy equal to 87 ounces of gas.*

• Use plastic berry baskets as refrigerator organizers.

• A wooden toy chest makes a wonderful bin for potatoes and onions.

• Use mesh potato bags as containers to hold loose lids and small pieces of dinnerware in your dishwasher.

• Fill a mustard squirt container with icing and use it to decorate cakes.

• To make a temporary cooler-to-go from a brown paper bag, insulate it with a folded newspaper.

• Use an older chest of drawers (painted or stained to match your cabinets) in your kitchen for linens, towels, or silverware storage.

• A plastic milk jug with the top cut off makes a wonderful scoop for pet food or for scooping out fertilizer from those big bags.

> **Recycling Fact:** *Americans throw away enough office paper each day to build a 12-foot-high wall of paper from New York to Los Angeles.*

• When baby grows up, move the diaper-changing table to the bathroom to hold towels and toiletries. Add a mirror over the changing table, and it will look even better.

• Use plastic breath-mint boxes to hold needles, pins, or pills when traveling.

- Save the seed packets as you plant your garden. They are great for country craft projects.

- Reuse envelopes from junk mail for scratch paper and grocery lists.

- Save empty film canisters, fill them with small objects, then glue them shut. They make great cat toys.

- Make emergency sewing kits from old matchbook covers. Use a rubber band to hold the thread and needles in.

- An old laundry basket is a perfect temporary dog bed (cut out one side).

- Use old metal shower curtain rings as key chains.

Maintenance

- Screen door squeak driving you crazy and no W-D-40? Try a non-stick vegetable spray!

- Petroleum jelly solves the problem of a sticking sliding door when you rub some of it on the track and move the door back and forth to evenly distribute the jelly.

- Door sticking? A reader from the cold area of Michigan sent this one in: Rub a bar of soap on the side of your door and it won't stick anymore.

- Clear fingernail polish put on the back of a loose cabinet knob will help it stay while you screw it back in.

Recycling Facts: *Recycling one ton of newspaper saves 17 trees.*

- Rubbing a pencil lead around the edges of your key makes unlocking doors easier.

Office/Workspace

- Take the labels off clean tin cans. Cover the cans with contact paper, and group them in various sizes as containers for pencils, pens, and miscellaneous items for a desk or bookshelf.

A Woman's Story

During the summer when the lawnmower was broken and wouldn't run, I kept hinting to my husband that he ought to get it fixed, but the message never sunk in. Finally, I thought of a clever way to make my point. When my husband arrived home that day, he found me seated in the tall grass snipping away busily with a tiny pair of sewing scissors. He watched silently for a short time, then went into the house. He was gone only a few minutes, and when he came out again he handed me a toothbrush. "When you finish cutting the grass," he said, "you might as well sweep the sidewalks."

- Use the frame of an old swing set to hang a hammock.

- People throw away perfectly good suitcases! Watch for them to make into decoupaged storage containers.

- Reuse cereal and detergent boxes. Cut off the tops of the boxes diagonally and decorate. Use it to hold files and magazines.

- Old and outdated napkin holders make super card or bill organizers.

- Almost anything can be turned into a desk. Concrete blocks and a door, a board and two smaller tables, filing cabinets, or stacked milk crates. Or purchase a kitchen table at a yard sale and decorate it as you like. You'll have plenty of room to work. Use your tightwad imagination.

- Save paper towel tubes for storing special drawings or pictures.

- Cut the corners off used envelopes and use as photo corners in your albums. (Those pretty-colored envelopes can be really fun to use for this!)

Outside Ideas

- Got a dead lawnmower? Remove the motor and top and replace it with a flat board to make a cart on wheels for moving items around the garden.

Recycling Fact: If every newspaper was recycled, it would save 250 million trees.

- Old handbags without shoulder straps make nice cosmetic traveling bags. Old handbags with straps make super tool bags that you can carry on your shoulder or hang it on the ladder.

- Old pantyhose makes wonderful ties for holding up tomato plants. Wet weather makes them even stronger.

- For a small watering system, punch tiny holes in a cut-off milk jug, fill with water, and place in a garden.

- Broken clay pots can be added to a garden wreath decorated with raffia or bits of pretty cloth.

- Save those coffee cans for storing nails, tools, and other small objects.

- A good emergency pet carrier for your car is two laundry baskets—one tied atop the other one.

- Glue multicolored old buttons to a straw hat to make a fun hat.

- An old burn barrel with a rack on top (from an old oven) makes a wonderful grill or smoker.

- Wooden pallets make a good garden fence in a pinch.

- A barrel filled with rocks or sand that has a hole in the middle of the top makes a great little outdoor table. Put a patio umbrella in the hole.

- Form a large circle with bricks, stacking them three high. Place an old oven rack or grate on the top, and you have a barbecue pit!

- Use a pair of old pantyhose over your hand to remove the bugs from your car.

- Use milk jugs or similar containers for little greenhouses or to protect small plants from the cold.

- Save those pizza boxes as forms for concrete. Create steppingstones to your garden (or weed patch!).

- Line plastic berry baskets with plastic wrap and use to plant seeds or starter plants.

- Old planks make great garage shelves. Look for bricks, also. Old bed slats are also good because they are uniform in size.

- Cut off the top half of a two-liter bottle and recycle it. Punch three holes along the top edges of the bottom. Poke a few small holes in the bottom. Then add dirt, tie up with twine, and use for a hanging plant container.

- An old garden shovel or rake, hand-held size, can be decorated with bits of clay pots, raffia, and seed packets and hung on the wall.

- Weatherproof TV trays make great patio tables.

- A wide, thick board atop two barrels or heavy-duty flower pots makes a perfect bench.

- Make outdoor chairs by cutting out L-shapes in large tree logs to form seats. Make some tables, too, by standing thick logs upright.

- To make an inexpensive table, top a clean garbage container or a large basket with a round or square piece of wood. Drape or paint. Great for storage, too.

- Gather construction flats or wooden forklift pallets for a simple patio floor.

- Deer don't like pantyhose or pet hair!! The next time you get your dog groomed, ask the groomer to save your dogs' hair for you. Place it in a pair of pantyhose, tie it up, and put in your garden. Deer will not come.

4

Calico Curtains and a Coat of Fresh Paint

Fast and Easy Decorating Tips

Our Mama was a great seamstress; she must have sewed dozens of curtains, dresses, and slipcovers for our family over the years. We often joked that if anyone sat still for more than 30 minutes in our house, Mama might cover them with calico or gingham. "Cozies" were her specialty. From Kleenex boxes, to kitchen mixers, to toilet paper—they all had matching, miniature slipcovers. Doilies, too, adorned every shelf, tabletop, and available furniture arm. No naked appliances or boxed toiletries in our house!

Mama went to be with the Lord in 1974. In 1980, Ann and I (Susan) happened to be going through an old box with my grandmother when we came upon a quilt wrapped in soft, yellowed tissue. Now our grandmother was a very modern lady, not nearly as home-spun and old-fashioned as our Mama. Grandma had actually stored the quilt away because she preferred to decorate with only the most modern items. When we saw the materials that were used in Mama's quilt, we sat down and ran our fingers along the multicolored, multitextured pattern with wonder and remembrance.

"Grandma," Ann finally said, "don't you see what a treasure this is? This little square is from our corduroy dresses, and here's the pink flannel from our pajamas, and look at the beautiful reds from our Christmas dresses!"

I pointed to a vintage fabric of dark yellow roses on a brown background. "Ann, here's our playhouse's kitchen curtains!"

"And our doll dresses!" Ann echoed, suddenly feeling six again.

Nightgowns, Easter dresses, a swatch from our prom formals...it was all there.

We took the quilt from Grandma's house that day and I (Susan) had the honor of putting it on display in my bedroom. I decorated my room a deep hunter green and red to match the Christmas colors sprinkled throughout the quilt.

Like our mother, we have a fondness for hand-made items, not only because it's a way to save money, but also because we appreciate the care that goes into a gift created with ingenuity and love. When we were young and time was plentiful, Mama taught us to crochet and knit. We loved making slippers and scarves and sweaters. Though free time is in short supply these days, our houses are still filled with hand-made decorations that were inexpensive and quick to create. We are old-fashioned women with old-fashioned decorating tastes. (We just want that lived-in, laid-back, antique look in a hurry!) Here are some of our favorite decorating discoveries!

Bedrooms

- A pointed picket fence headboard is really cute when painted to look like color pencils or crayons.

• Line a drawer with non-skid shelf paper or a piece of remnant carpet and put jewelry in it. No scratches and your pieces stay put!

• Create an illusion of a headboard using small pictures in a design to simulate a headboard.

• Hide those perfumed sniffer-strips found in magazines in your bathroom or other rooms for a delightful smell.

• Loop plastic six pack rings over hangers to make more room for hanging clothes up.

• Drooling over those gorgeous padded headboards? Make one yourself with a board, fabric, an old blanket for a "filler sack," and nails. Wrap as you would a gift and tack or pin together.

• Got a pretty wooden towel rack? Hang securely above your bed, then loop your favorite afghan or quilt on the rack. (You'll need to hang the rack pretty close to the ceiling to adjust for length of your blanket.)

• Almost anything that you have discovered can become a headboard—an old gate, ironwork, or a weathered board.

• A bookshelf makes a wonderful headboard for a bed and frame. Just nail it on the wall the right height for the bed.

> *"If you stop to be kind you*
> *must swerve often from your path."*
> *—Mary Webb*

- Ask your video store for their movie posters when they are done using them. Also, the grocery store throws away a lot of visual aids such as flowers and cut-out pictures. Teenagers and kids love these for decorations.

- Want more drama for your four-poster bed? Simply tie a fabric sheer on each post and swag it loosely.

- A great-looking, creative room does not have to be hard to do. Just think outside the normal lines. For example, for a Dalmatian puppy theme, dip your thumb and three fingers in black paint and "walk" them across the walls, ceiling, closets, or furniture to create little paw prints all around.

- Gather fabric in a top knot with a rubber band. Cover rubber band with a ribbon. Hang on wall and drape the fabric around the head of a bed for a headboard.

- To create a boxed-in-bed look, paint, then nail short 2 x 4 boards on the ceiling to form four L-shaped corners. Staple or nail on your bed fabric and let it hang. (A sheet works nicely.)

- Two rods positioned above your bed, one right at the top of your ceiling and wall joint and the other on the ceiling about halfway out over the bed, are perfect to drape a flat piece of material through for a unique headboard. Start at the floor behind your bed and go upward over both rods.

Creating Ambiance and Style

- Old shutters hinged together make an adorable screen to hide the fireplace in the summer.

- Cover children's dresser drawers by gluing on comic strip paper. Cover the paper with a coat of white glue mixed with water to protect it.

- Find an old ottoman at a garage sale. Cover it with any material you have on hand (a piece of an old quilt would be adorable for a country look) and use decorative thumb tacks or nails to attach the fabric. You may need to unscrew the legs first.

- Need a magazine rack for the bathroom? Use a towel rack of any kind and hang the magazine open, face down.

- A simple bow at the base of a candle holder adds an interesting touch.

- A pretty tray can make a nice tabletop.

- A very large vase makes a useful umbrella/cane holder.

- Wooden Coke crates make great plant "wagons"—and so does your child's old red wagon!

- A stepladder makes a great plant stand.

- Be imaginatively different in your tablecloth selections. Look around the house—what about a shawl, a giant scarf, or a sheet?

- Top a large vase with a round glass or wood top for a decorative corner table.

- Glue cardboard checkerboards onto tables. Varnish or decoupage and you have a wonderful game table.

- Using thumbtacks, create a design along the side of an upholstered chair to create more interest.

- Any jar can make a cute vase or button holder or candy jar if you add a scrap of lace and pretty ribbon.

- An old lamp comes alive by setting it on pretty material, then gathering it around the base in an upward sweep and tying it with raffia or ribbon at the neck (below the bulb base and switch area). Make sure the cloth isn't too close to the bulb.

- Antique your dresser drawers by painting on a layer of glue over the dry paint. It will dry crackly!

- Do you love the look of those fake country brown eggs? (They look so cute in a country bowl, but they can be expensive.) Buy a dozen real brown eggs, poke pin holes in either end and blow out the eggs. (Kids love this!) Line 'em up on the back porch in their swimming suits in the summertime, and let them blow the eggs. They give you the shells, and you can let them have an egg-slime fight. You'll give them a memory they'll never forget. It's good to surprise and shake kids up every so often by being a crazy, fun mom. (And you can just wash the kids down with a hose when it's over.) Arrange the shells in a nest for a pretty centerpiece.

- Cut off a short section of a log and carve out a small hole with a pocket knife. This is a great rustic candlestick.

- Put a rubber band around a candle before putting it in your candle holder. It will help it stay upright.

- For that country look, roll balls of colorful rag strips and balls of twine and place in an old basket.

• Save those big plaster and paint buckets from construction sites and decorate with contact paper, stickers, or paint them. Use for wastebaskets, containers for children's toys (depending on previous contents), barbecue charcoal containers (with the lid on it will keep that leftover charcoal nice and dry), or umbrella stands.

• People who hire workers to construct a new backyard fence usually throw away the pieces of old fencing. You can hinge them to make a great "cowboy" room divider.

• Contact paper cut-outs of your children's hands make a great ceiling border. Wouldn't it be a great idea to start your child's hand collection on a door or a wall and, each year, have your child add new prints? Watch that hand grow!

• For a unique flower pot stand, place one large, empty flower pot upside down and one pot with the flowers in it on top of the bottom pot.

• Use interesting items for drawer handles such as beads on a string, silverware, or blocks.

• Even small swatches of lace glued to a lampshade can look pretty. You can also add old buttons or charms for an old-fashioned look.

• Find a piece of an old picket fence or pretty gate to put in front of your fireplace in the summer time. Decorate with sprigs of real or fake ivy. Or use a solid piece of painted wood, wrapped and tied with ribbons.

• Need two bookcases? Cut a used, tall bookcase in half and add boards to make new sides. Add some paint and you have like-new bookcases you can turn any way you want!

- When is it okay to color and scribble on a wall? When you need a really unique focal wall in a kid's playroom. You can buy a can of blackboard paint as a base, then let the kids go crazy with colored chalk.

- Buy thrift-store or dollar-store pearls and arrange them in crystal bowls or fancy glasses around a wedding table for an elegant touch.

- Use wallpaper borders to emphasize a small area or focal wall. A plain mirror or window perks right up with a wallpaper border as a frame.

- Decorate plain lampshades by gluing on a button trim. Four painted dots around each button makes a nice flower design.

- If you can't afford painted tiles, buy decals and put them on plain tiles.

- Make new fabric old by dying it with strong tea. This is a nice effect for curtains or tablecloths—and perfect for salvaging white tablecloths that have been stained.

- Save that piece of lace to drape over a colored tablecloth. Instant elegance!

Decorating with Colors and Textures

- Want to color the mood in your home? Scientists have discovered that red generates energy, yellow builds creativity, green brings a feel of nature, blue calms, and purple is regal and classy.

- Red is great for an accent color, especially in the kitchen. It stimulates the appetite and the mood and flow of the conversation. Bright yellow can be stimulating. Use it in a room where you are working to keep up your visual energy and creativity. Black in your home is much like a simple black dress. It can be elegant or depressing. Use it with bright colors or white to keep the mood upbeat. Green helps with the concentration level...great for a home office. This is why some offices have an abundance of plants. Blue is great for a bedroom because it promotes calmness.

- Use colors like oranges, reds, and browns to create warmth. "Cool" a warm, sunny room with colors like ivy green, lavender, or slate blue.

- Stripes and checks make a formal room a little cozier. Velvets and silks formalize a room even a few pieces will have a dramatic effect.

- If your ceilings are low, paint the walls, moldings, and ceiling the same color. Emphasize the beauty of high ceilings by painting them a different color than the walls.

- Bright colors, added as accents to an all-white room, really look great—almost like power bursts of color. If you're on a budget, start with classic white as a background.

- It's cheaper to paint older appliances than to buy new ones. There is now special appliance paints (some are heat resistant) in your local stores if you need to cover up that old harvest gold or avocado green. (Of course, just as soon as you do those colors will probably come back into style!)

- Silver and gold are cheap—in spray paint, that is. Use these colors to add a classy touch to anything.

- Real leaves make great natural "stamps." Dip lightly in paint and press to make a design for a border, lampshade, or decoration.

- Hold fall leaves together tightly around a small clear glass and tie with a gold or red ribbon. Insert a candle.

- Forget the needle and thread—use diaper pins to "wrap" a foam cushion with material. Change it when you're bored with it.

- Want to fancy up a plain basket? Weave in colorful ribbon or paint a design using the weave as your guide. Add a bow on top if you like.

- Use a hair pick for creating a design the next time you paint a wall. Run the pick down the wall. Plastic bags crumpled and dipped in paint also make interesting wall patterns.

- Forget buying brass pots; paint any kind of pot gold or brass (dull or bright).

- If you can't afford painted tiles, choose a few fancy tiles to arrange in a unique pattern among inexpensive tiles.

- For drawer handles, be creative! Use baby blocks, small balls, and old doorknobs.

- If you want a wainscoting look in your room, pick a floral print (or another wallpaper design that isn't going to be a hassle to match) and place on your wall horizontally. Saves time in cutting, and your wallpaper just keeps on going around. Add plastic or wood molding or a wallpaper border on top of the wainscoting. So fast and easy we almost felt like we were cheating when we did this!

- You can cut your own stencils from pieces of plastic that usually get thrown away—stars, moons, and leaves are all easy shapes to cut out with a razor knife. Use them as patterns for painting borders, decorating bedrooms, or jazzing up small spaces.

- Paint an ugly chair many different colors—perhaps a yellow seat, red arms, blue back, with black polka dots. Think "Mary Englebreit" and let your whimsical side have fun! Many pieces like this are selling for lots of money in craft and antique malls.

- Found a good buy on decorative wide ribbon? Use it as a border around the ceiling. Any valance can be made better by adding two ribbons (dividing the valance into thirds) and tying them tightly to bring up the curtain in a scalloped effect.

- Tie two bandannas together at the corners to cover a tired pillow.

- Can't afford expensive patio tile to hide ugly concrete? Get out some masking tape and outdoor spray paint and design your own spray-on-tile. This works great on a porch, and there are so many faux paint treatments available now that can give it a nice authentic look.

- Consider using primary colors in the nursery instead of pastels. These colors can "grow" with a child easier than "infant pastels," which will save you decorating money.

- A simple candle placed in a small glass jar becomes special when decorated with leaves and raffia.

- Tie a knot at all four corners of a bandanna or handkerchief and use to cover a container for a plant. Lay it on the table, place a pot in the center, then bring the cloth up around the pot and secure with a rubber band. The four knotted corners will be heavy enough to hang down and hide the rubber band.

• Change your floors. There are paints made especially for floor, decks, and porches. Simply roll it on! Use a sponge or crumpled up plastic bags and blotch on the paint to give the floor a nice texture. A polyurethane coating will also revitalize a floor that has seen better days.

Pictures, Frames, and Wall-Hangings

• Upholstery tacks come in an assortment of colors, shapes, and designs. Use them to trim picture frames, mirrors, or on a door. They give an instant touch of elegance.

• Paint six or more pinch-type clothespins and glue onto a painted board. Great for hanging up potholders and coupons, and adds a clean, crisp decoration to your kitchen. Makes a convenient message board for the family, too.

• Hang your hats on the wall to create a decorative collection. When you want to wear a hat, just pick it off the wall.

• A piece of an old quilt can be used in a pretty, inexpensive picture frame (try a large one!) as a beautiful wall decoration.

• Use old drawer knobs fixed to a wall or board as a place to hang jackets, towels, umbrellas, canes, and so on.

• Create your own decorative light switch plates. Splatter paint them, then add decorative stickers, leftover wallpaper borders, or contact paper.

• Group a variety of family photos in picture frames together on a table or mantel for a very pretty, homey look.

• Magazine advertisements are gorgeous to use in collages on wood, boxes, or mirrors. Some pages are beautiful enough to frame for a special decorative touch. Perfume ads have gorgeous floral patterns that can be cut out and used to cover a box or tabletop for a lovely Victorian look. We framed doll advertisements to brighten our daughters' rooms.

• Hot glue a pretty bow above a framed picture, tucking two ribbon "tails" behind the frame. It looks like the picture is actually hanging by the bow—a very charming effect.

• Don't forget that paper-and-hanger mobiles and simple kites make great inexpensive decorations. Hang them from the ceiling if you want!

• A little twine clothesline mounted on a country wall looks cute with tiny little socks or clothes hung "to dry." (You can find adorable miniature working clothespins in dollar stores.) How about this in your laundry room, above your backdoor or window, or as a wall border?

• Watch for good deals on pictures with frames at yard sales. Don't just look at the print—if the frame is in good shape, buy it!

• Spray paint the various frames you have collected in one color to create a unified grouping.

• Any board and a few nails (to use as hooks) makes an instant coat rack, hat rack, purse rack, or hanger for book bags and skates.

- Save your fabric scraps and even your old clothes to make rag tags, then tie around a wire coat hanger stretched out to make a wreath. Add some everyday items such as spools, flowers, little wooden cows or pigs, and you'll soon have the cutest homespun wreath.

- Use rustic twine or cord to wrap around an ugly frame. (You'll have to remove the picture and glass for this.)

- Gather small sticks and pieces of twigs that bend. Bend to form half hearts, then tie together with raffia. This makes a great hearth decoration.

- An old wreath becomes new by adding items such as artificial fruits, birds, children's blocks (for a nursery)—anything you have saved from gifts or wrappings.

- Spray paint an old broom handle and place on top of a two hooks lengthwise on a wall. Use as a quilt rack!

Window Treatments

- A plain muslin curtain (or white or cream sheet) looks colorful and cheerful when you let the kids decorate it with fabric paint.

- An inexpensive little wreath makes a unique curtain tie-back.

- Poofy curtains to the rescue! Never underestimate the power of a little rubber band when creating those "poof ball" curtains. Use rubber bands around the curtain and fluff material near the top near your rod. Continue using rubber bands to create as many poofs as you like. Or, if you have long drapes, slip the rubber band to the center of the drape and poof the upper part to cover the rubber band until you have the length that you desire.

- An old key or a large nail placed in the hems of your curtains keeps them hanging straight.

- Fix old drawer knobs on each end of a board nailed atop a window. Drape a piece of sheer fabric over the knobs for an easy-to-install window treatment.

- Use pretty dish towels to cover that window in a kitchen backdoor or your laundry room. Cut vertical slits near the top and bottom hems at one-inch intervals. Weave the towel onto the dowels and attach them to the top and bottom of the window.

- Keep an eye out for old windows with interesting sections. Use as a frame for country scenes, tack lace behind it, or put over a mirror. Great to hide an ugly wall section or simply to add a nice window treatment to the decor.

- Use napkins, scarves, or bandannas, folded in half with points downward (like a row of banners) for a quick and pretty valance.

- An instant valance: Make two fabric bows and place them at each upper end of a window. Hot glue a clothespin just under each bow (so it doesn't show). Use a light-weight piece of your favorite fabric and drape and clothespin it into place across the top of the window.

- No drapery or shower curtain hooks? Use twine or cord and string from the first hole to the last by looping over the rod and in and out of each hole. Color coordinate the cord with your curtain.

- A lace valance is easy to hang—simply loop the rod through the lace holes.

- To widen your window wall without remodeling, hang a drapery rod between two windows and extend it over window length. Hang your drapes over that. No one will guess that there are two small windows there instead of four!

- No curtain rod? Hang your country curtain over a taut piece of twine or attach it with little clothespins.

- Do you have an heirloom tablecloth with a stain? Fold or cut so the stain won't show and use as a curtain.

- This is a super tightwad trick for outdoor shutters. If you can't afford to buy real shutters, buy the "snap-together" flowerbed fences. Nail to the window sides, with the edges pointing *away* from the window and you have shutters. They usually come in hunter green or white and look great on the house!

5

Creative Gifts and Holiday Tips

Having Fun on a Budget

Birthdays and holidays—especially Christmas—were cele-brated wholeheartedly at the Fox house. And we've carried forth the tradition of joyful thanksgiving to share with our kids. The delights of giving—and, we'll admit, the wonders of receiving—are repeated as much as possible in our homes as we celebrate our lives and the wonderful love and grace of our Savior, Jesus Christ.

We especially remember the big family picture Bible that was always open to the story of Jesus' birth during the Christmas season. We loved winding up the little church that would light up and play "Silent Night." One of our greatest joys was running to the living room to see what was in our stockings. (In the tightwad tra-dition, our stockings were really Daddy's socks in disguise!) We were thrilled to discover—and eat—the bright red-and-white candy canes, wonderful freshly cracked walnuts, and the deliciously sweet oranges.

Along with healthy doses of love and laughter, the following tips and ideas will help you create special occasions and isn't-it-a-glorious-day parties that your family and friends will cherish forever!

Entertaining

- For quick and pretty table decorating, loosely knot cloth napkins and slip the silverware through the knot. Why have napkins rings?

- Love those two- or three-tier crystal or fancy dessert dishes on a buffet table? Make your own by topping a crystal pedestal bowl with a flat crystal plate, then another pedestal bowl, and so on.

- Orange peels in a pot of boiling water will fill your house with the delightful aroma of walking into an orchard.

- Get a large chunk of ice for your punchbowl by freezing water in a large margarine tub. If you leave room at the top for expansion, you can plop the lid on top to keep the ice from absorbing fridge odors. (Also makes a nice cold pack should somebody sprain their backs carrying the punch bowl....)

- Store bags of ice in your washing machine, dishwasher, or bathtub. They make great ice chests, and are handy when you have a lot of company.

- Rejuvenate your potpourri by spraying a little air freshener into the bowl.

- Party centerpieces: To create festive, small centerpieces for a long or large table, insert small flags into white paper cups filled with gumdrops. These make great party favors, too.

Gift Giving

- Here's a great gift idea: NBA Fan-Mail packages. Order a fan-mail package for your friend's or child's favorite basketball team. Packages include team decals and photos of the team stars. Send a business size SASE to the following of your choice: Atlanta Hawks, Public Relations Dept., ONE CNN Center #405, Atlanta, GA 30303; Boston Celtics, Attn: Fan Mail Dept., 151 Merrimac St., 5th Floor, Boston, MA 02114; Chicago Bulls, 980 N. Michigan Avenue, Room #1600, Chicago, IL 60611-4501.

- Shop for gifts at stores that gift wrap for free.

- See-through plastic boxes and containers can be lined with tissue paper or potpourri and filled with a few little gifts. Tie closed with big colorful ribbons. These boxes can be purchased for less than a dollar at craft stores—much cheaper than most store-bought gift bags, and they have a much longer and useful life.

- Make a master list for Christmas and use it each year to organize your gift ideas.

- As you find little gifts for your kid's stocking stuffers, place them in a paper bag and label it. (If your kids might peek, label it "vitamins" or "dried spinach" to keep them from getting their goodies too early.)

> ***Recycling Fact:*** *The average person uses 600 pounds of paper per year.*

- If you don't make your own gifts, at least make life easier by ordering from a catalog and having the company mail it to the person you are giving it to.

- If you must buy gift wrap, buy a design that you can use for multiple holidays and purposes. Gold, silver, and white are the most versatile colors.

- Make your own greeting cards from note cards and postcards. If you own a computer you have all you need to personalize a card for any occasion.

- Use colored cellophane to present your homemade gifts to someone. Cut off the tops, twist the tops, or bend the tops over for different looks.

- Send Christmas postcards instead of cards to save on postage and paper waste. You can cut off the front half of a used Christmas card and turn it into an instant holiday postcard!

- If you have to mail gifts, consider giving gift certificates.

- Hot chocolate and spice-tea mixes are great gifts. Place them in a pretty mug, tie a ribbon on the handle, and offer your friends a "moment to sip and sit and be thankful."

- Americans bought over $450,000 worth of gift wrap in 1996 and sent over 2 billion Christmas cards. Pinking sheers, several rubber stamps, colored stamp pads, paper, and sacks are all you need to create your own cards, gift wrap, and gift bags.

- Wrap a bottle of nonalcoholic wine with a piece of fabric or a cloth napkin and tie with a ribbon before giving it as a gift.

- A plain meat loaf pan can be made special by making a design using a hammer and a nail, then filling it with homemade goodies with a red ribbon tied around it. The pan can then be hung on the wall for decoration.

- Cover that homemade gift from the oven with those beautiful designer paper towels.

- To wrap an oversized present, use a green or white trash bag tied with a red ribbon.

- For holiday savings, keep your shopping list with you all of the time. Impulsive buying or not sticking to your list costs you more money.

- For holidays and special occasions, buy one nice gift for a couple or for an entire family when possible. It's cheaper and less time-consuming—and is usually more appreciated.

- A clean waste can makes an excellent portable gift-wrapping supply holder.

- After the holidays, buy holiday cards and gift wrap at half price to use next year.

- A plain brown bag can become a quaint country gift bag by adding a square swatch of red-checked or print fabric and a few buttons.

- Make a cute birthday bow for a child by using gum stick wrappers connected in the middle with a piece of candy, all held together by a pipe cleaner.

- Brown lunch bags look great stamped with gold images and decorated with a gold bow for a quick gift wrap!

- Reuse the liner in cereal and snack boxes. The silver ones, after being rinsed and dried, make nice holiday gift bags. Just tie with a bright ribbon, and no one will know that your Snap, Crackle, Pop® provided you with glitz, sparkle, and joy.

- A piece of lace draped over a jar, with the lid holding the lace in place, is great for presenting homemade goodies. This also makes a wonderful accent in your room. *Note:* Works best if you first cut the lace into large circles that will cover the jar.

- How about a gift wreath for a friend who is a cook? Save that old wreath that you were thinking of throwing away and add some wooden spoons, can labels, forks—anything else you can get your hands on in the kitchen besides the kitchen sink.

- Make your own unique envelopes or foldable gift boxes! Carefully take apart a regular envelope or box and lay it out as a pattern. Trace the pattern onto paper and cut out. You can use maps, wallpaper, children's school papers—the ideas are as endless as the type of paper around us.

- Save your peanut butter jars and other large-mouthed containers to use for gift packages of cookies and candies. Add a piece of fabric and a ribbon over the top. The plastic containers (and Pringles® cans) are wonderful for sending care packages to college kids or grandchildren.

- Save shampoo and makeup samples to tuck into a gift basket for a friend or keep a little toiletry basket for company. Such a nice gesture.

- Get a colorful permanent marking pen for writing on slick gift wrapping. You won't have to buy gift tags!

- Store your gift wrapping and gift tags and ribbons in a hanging garment bag.

- Glue sticks are a good alternative to tape when gift wrapping.

- Popped popcorn makes excellent packing material.

Holiday Decorations

- Let the kids thread Styrofoam® packing "peanuts" into "snowy" Christmas garlands.

- Save your bits of fabric to make a rag wreath or garland. Simply tie six to eight strips of fabric to twine or yarn and tie a knot for each one. For a wreath, push little fabric squares into a Styrofoam® form. Also, try bending a hanger for a heart-shaped form.

> *God put us on earth to accomplish a certain number of things. Right now, we're so far behind, we will live forever.*

- Make your own miniature reindeer using twigs for antlers and tiny logs for the body and head.

- Use a hole punch and a Phillips screwdriver to create a design on a dark-colored lampshade. Looks great when turned on at night. How about punching in your child's name or designing a holiday motif in your favorite holiday lamp?

> *Buying and budgeting require organization so "plan that work and work that plan" ladies!*

- A white tablecloth comes alive with this fun, quick drape: Weave colored ribbons and drape loosely over the tablecloth. Match your ribbon colors with the holiday or festivity.

- Buy one grapevine wreath and decorate it for your front door; redecorate it for different seasons or holidays.

- An old paperback book, pages turned halfway down diagonally and the front and back covers glued together, painted green, becomes a tabletop tree. Add a bow or star to the top.

- Make your own fireplace mantel "snow" by cutting white poster paper into the shape of dripping snow. Tape it around the edge of the mantel.

- Don't have a heart-shaped cookie cutter? Take a clean tuna can and cut out the top and bottom. Then press into a heart or any other shape.

- Make a button wreath by gluing buttons onto a circular piece of cardboard or poke with pins into a Styrofoam® wreath. Add a ribbon for color.

- Wrap Christmas fragiles in a light bulb sleeve and box.

- Company coming and you need a little Christmas cheer right this very minute? Run outside and find a small log. Nail streams of red ribbon and bells to it, and you have an instant "Welcome" door decoration.

• Gumdrops on toothpicks, stuck into a Styrofoam® ball makes a great edible ball for a holiday decoration. Add a ribbon to hang.

• Cut out a gingerbread man garland using brown paper bags. Attach to a Christmas ribbon and hang.

• Stack and glue empty thread spools upwards, beginning with 4 at the bottom, then 3, then 2 and then 1. Spray paint them green. Decorate with painted-on ornaments or buttons for a little Christmas tree country style.

• Twist brown paper bags into a nice brown wreath shape. Attach candy canes to the paper wreath with red pipe cleaners. Add a huge red ribbon or bow.

• Wrap a piece of lace you have saved around the base of a candle for an elegant touch.

• Tall bottles, especially green ones, make great candle holders for red candles at Christmas.

• Save the branches of an old artificial Christmas tree and make wreaths by adding pine cones and little treasures (small toys, buttons, old ornaments). Top with a big bow.

• Felt is still the cheapest and easiest way to make holiday banners and decorations.

• Hang pine cones from red ribbons for a beautiful, natural Christmas look in your yard. You don't want partridges in a bare tree!

• A plain, tan doormat becomes festive by spray-painting a tree stencil around the edges. (You can cut simple triangle stencils out of a piece of thin cardboard.)

- A pretty lace handkerchief draped over a small ball (for the head) and secured with ribbon around the neck makes a nice angel for a Christmas tree or a decoration for a present to a friend.

- A day-old loaf of bread can make a cute, country-style multicandle holder. Punch in candlesticks evenly along the length of the bread.

- Place a votive candle on a little melted wax inside half an orange peel. The aroma will be wonderful.

- Scoop out a small portion of the top of some red apples, insert some green candles and add a plaid ribbon or some bells for Christmas. Make sure the candles and apples are sturdy and won't tip over.

- A sprig of holly, evergreen, or flowers tied to the back of a chair is a great decoration. (*Hint:* Why wait for holidays? Use this idea for birthday parties and wedding receptions.)

- Are you artistically challenged when making a jack-o-lantern? After cutting the top off and removing the seeds of a pumkin, punch holes in a pattern with a large nail. When the light shines through you will have a beautiful punched-tin effect!

- Liven up a dessert tray or just decorate a table piling red apples with candy canes in a country basket.

Housework can kill you,
so why take a chance?
—Phyllis Diller

- No candle holders? Create a decorative arrangement using a bowl filled with popcorn and evergreens. Use pine cones to hold the candles snugly.

- A glass or silver bowl is classy filled with shiny Christmas balls. Surrounded by bright lights, it is beautiful.

- An orange tied with red ribbon is simple, but pretty. Use your imagination and create a unique effect by using several ribbons on one orange.

- Cut out wrapping paper in various sizes of rectangles and squares. Arrange them on your front door with Sticky Tack so they look like stacks of gift-wrapped boxes. Add sticky bows and you've got a holiday door ready to welcome in the world!

- Raffia tied in the middle with red ribbon makes a wonderful decoration on the door, mantel, on inside doors—and makes a great mistletoe holder. Use the raffia later with another ribbon for everyday decor.

- Plastic Christmas tablecloths make a perfect tree skirt. Simply cut a slit to the center of the cloth and wrap around the tree.

- Used, big, decorative popcorn tins make unique decorations for the corner on your porch.

6

Saving Energy and Spring Cleaning

Mama's Cleaning Tips and Energy Savers

The click-swish-click-swoosh of Mama's mop coming down the green tiled hall (surplus tiles from the school system) was as much a part of the background sounds of our childhood as the coffeepot perking or the attic fan humming. It signaled that late afternoon had arrived and was melting toward evening. It also said that Daddy would be coming home from work soon. Mama was a fastidious housekeeper and insisted that our home look tidy each evening for Dad's arrival.

And it was.

Unless, that is, you happened to open a cabinet or pull out a drawer. Mama was an incredible "stuffer." But the surface—what company saw—was always spotless.

Even Mama's clothes were remarkably neat. She wore crisp shirtwaist dresses, always covered with a freshly starched apron.

(Picture Donna Reed or June Cleaver, then subtract the pearls and heels and you've got Mama.) She would often say, "One can be poor, but there's no excuse for not being clean because soap's cheap!"

Even the front yard had to meet up to her standards of cleanliness. When the leaves began to fall in the autumn, Mama would grab her rake and work gloves and head out the door, a steel glint in her eye, bent on conquering each afternoon's leaf invasion. One day she was raking leaves and bent down to light a pile of them with a match. To her amazement, the cover of a nearby manhole blew off with the force and sound of a rocket. The fire department even came to see what disaster had befallen our neighborhood. (The pile of leaves were too close to a natural gas line!) Thankfully no one was hurt, but still the story was big enough in a small town to be considered newsworthy. (Of course, a squirrel crossing the street could be considered an event in sleepy little southern towns.) Mama was mortified when she read of the happenings in the local paper the next day, but Daddy laughed about it for years.

> *Cleaning and scrubbing can wait*
> *'til tomorrow...for babies grow up,*
> *we've learned to our sorrow. So quiet down,*
> *cobwebs; dust, go to sleep...I'm rocking my*
> *baby, and babies don't keep.*

With a neatnik Mama, one might think we twins would both have been cut out of Mama's tidy mold. However, just because Susan and I (Ann) are twins, doesn't mean we are the same in every way. Susan was, shall I say, more "relaxed" about neatness than I was. I was downright obsessive-compulsive about being organized, and when I'd glance over at Susan's side of the room and spy her mounting hill of clothes on the floor, the bed, under the bed, hanging from her dresser and off her lampshade, I'd see red. We used to have fights over the state of our room; we'd get so worked up and angry. Thankfully, when our brother and sister married, Susan and I each received a room of our own. The whole family rejoiced, knowing the noise level in the household would subside several notches.

Mama was always soft spoken and calm. Except one particular day that none of us can forget. It was really the only time we can remember our kind-hearted mother losing her cool. The old wringer washer, decades past its youth, sprung a leak, and proceeded to water the floor of the kitchen, living room, and a bedroom. Mother picked up the phone, dialed Daddy and went berserk. He was so surprised by her outburst since they were such a rarity that all he could do was laugh—and make sure she got a new washing machine the next day.

Our big sister, Char, was even more orderly than I (Ann) was. Susan and I knew that to enter the sanctum of her room was to put our mortal lives in danger. In spite of our fear, one day we slipped into her room just to sit on her big, tall twin bed for a few minutes. Then the horrible, inevitable happened. We spilled black ink on her white chenille bedspread. That was 40 years ago, and she's still trying to find a way to forgive us.

Though Char and I come by the desire for a neat house quite honestly, we often envy Susan's ability to relax and enjoy life— even when there's a sink full of dishes that need to be washed. I often quote the nursery poem on the previous page. When my desire for cleanliness pushes against the need to enjoy my children and grandchildren. It's Susan's philosophy of childrearing.

So rock your baby first. Enjoy every second. But when you are done, put on your apron and get out your feather duster. We've got some fun tips to help you save on energy and zip through those cleaning jobs without spending too much time or too much money—whether you're a neatie or a messy!

Corralling the Energy Busters
Electrical and Gas

- Call your power company about a free energy audit. They may also insulate pipes and install low-flow shower heads at no charge.

- Use your crockpot and microwave to save on electricity. Plus your house doesn't heat up—especially important during the summer!

- Do you have one of those window air conditioners that drip water continuously? Set your watering can underneath or your pet's water bowl. Why waste water when this can save time. And your pet will never go thirsty!

- Run your dishwasher only when it is full. Turn off the "heat dry" button, and let the dishes air dry.

- Use a timer for morning showers. Keeps hot water-loving kids moving!

> *Be a kid again! Mow your grass with an old-fashioned push mower. (Have you ever pushed one of these things around the yard? If not, your grandparents probably did!) You get free exercise, little maintenance cost, and no gas to purchase or go and get. We're serious! Get moving!*

- If you lower your hot water heater setting by 15°, you will save more than two dollars per month. One hundred twenty degrees should be adequate. Lower the temperature when you go away on vacation.

- You use 9 gallons of water every time you wash dishes by hand. A dishwasher uses approximately 13 gallons.

- Fluorescent lights provide three times the light as incandescent for the same amount of electricity. They are very economical for bathrooms and kitchens, last ten times as long, and produce less heat.

- Dimmer switches can multiply bulb life up to 12 times, while reducing electricity usage.

- Turn lights off when you leave a room.

- Use lower watt bulbs.

- Move furniture away from vents and heating/cooling units.

- Vacuum the condenser coil of your refrigerator (below or at the back of it) three or four times a year. Clean coils keep it running efficiently and help save electricity.

- Vacuum heating filters often and spray them with furniture spray. You can do this two or three times a year before buying new ones. During winter months, however, replace them once a month.

- Limit the use of soap and the length of washing and drying cycles. Clothes only need a 10- to 15-minute wash cycle.

- The best water saver for the bathroom is a low-flow toilet that uses only 1.5 to 1.6 gallons. Eventually they pay for themselves by reducing water bills.

- The biggest waste of hot water in your home is the shower. Older shower heads deliver up to eight gallons per minute. Shop for a shower head that puts out three gallons or less per minute.

- Don't leave the water running while you brush your teeth, shave, or wash your face. Fill the sink rather than use a constant stream. This simple procedure can save your family as much as 2,000 gallons a year.

- Front-load washers use 33 percent less water than top-load washers.

- Don't wash a medium load on a higher water-level setting.

- A faucet aerator can cut water use in half and save up to 100 gallons a year per faucet. Aerators for kitchen and bath faucets can be found in most hardware stores. They cost between three and ten dollars and simply screw onto your faucet nozzle.

- Check for water system leaks. Before leaving on your next trip away from home, write down the numbers on your water meter when you leave. Check the meter again upon returning. If it has moved at all you have a leak, and you may be in over your head on your next water bill.

- Water your lawn and garden early in the morning. Watering during the day is less efficient due to water evaporation.

- Unplug your coffeepot, iron, electric skillet, and curling iron when you are finished using them.

- Vacuum the foam filters in your air conditioner every month. It will help with the cooling bill and the efficiency of your air conditioner.

- To save the maximum amount of water in your toilet, fill a half-gallon plastic milk jug with small rocks. Then fill with water. Place it in your tank away from the mechanism.

- Reuse your vacuum bag—it's still good, just empty it!

- For every mark above 65° (Fahrenheit) on your thermostat, you add 3 percent to your heating bill.

- Buy your air conditioners in February and March for big bargains.

- Use room and attic fans instead of air conditioning to cool your house whenever possible.

- A faucet that leaks 60 drops of water per minute wastes 168 gallons per month.

- In the summer, for every degree below 77° you set your air conditioner, you add 7 percent to your electricity bill.

- Need a gas hot water heater? Call your gas company. They have deals where you can get one for free or for very low cost.

Recycling

- If you have lost the negative to a picture that you'd like to reprint, most copying companies can make you an excellent color copy.

- In a hurry to get dressed and you discover a run in your nylons? On two pairs of pantyhose cut off the bad leg. Then insert the good leg of a pair inside the hole of the other pair, and you have a good pair of pantyhose. This is why it's good to always buy the same shade of pantyhose.

- Cut off the toes of old pantyhose and wear them on your toes underneath your regular hose and the toes lasts longer.

Getting Rid of the Nitty Gritty

Cleansers and Sprays That Work!

Note: Label these homemade cleansers when you place them in spray bottles or regular bottles or containers.

- *All-purpose household cleaner:* ½ cup white vinegar, 1 cup ammonia, ¼ cup baking soda, 1 gallon water.

- *Automatic dishwasher detergent:* 1 cup borax, ½ cup baking soda, 3 cups of cheap automatic dishwasher detergent.

- *Cleanser for garbage disposal:* 1 cup baking soda, 1¼ cups water. Mix ingredients and pour into ice cube trays and freeze. Turn on the disposal (no water running) and dump five to seven ice cubes down the drain, allowing the machine to grind them up.

- *Powdered carpet cleaner:* 2 cups baking soda, ½ cup cornstarch, 1 T. ground cloves. Sprinkle over the carpet to be cleaned, leave overnight, and vacuum as usual.

> *Cleaning your house while your kids are still growing is like shoveling the walk before it stops snowing.*
> —Phyllis Diller

- *Liquid carpet cleaner:* A good stain remover for carpet is laundry detergent, water, and white vinegar.

- *Laundry stain remover:* You can use a spray bottle for this one. ½ cup white vinegar, ½ cup ammonia, ½ cup store-bought liquid laundry soap, ½ cup water. Spray stain, rub in mixture, let garment sit for a bit, then wash.

- *Heavy-duty stain remover for fabrics:* Mix ½ cup dish-washing liquid, ½ cup baking soda, then add 1 gallon of boiling water. Let your clothes soak in this overnight if possible, and then wash as you usually would.

- *Basic cleaner:* To 1 gallon of hot water add 2 T. baking soda and ½ cup detergent.

- *Furniture polish:* Mix 1 part lemon juice and 2 parts vegetable oil. Dust as usual.

- *Toilet cleaner:* Vinegar will remove many rust stains because it is a natural acid. Also sprinkle baking soda into your toilet once or twice a month and let it stand overnight.

- *Glass cleaner:* 2 T. cornstarch and ½-cup white vinegar to 1 gallon of warm water. *Note:* Vinegar (even without the cornstarch) makes an excellent glass cleaner with a little water added. Use it as your car windshield cleaner.

- *Carpet deodorizer:* Sprinkle on baking soda, wait 7 to 10 minutes, then vacuum as usual.

- *Car wash mixture:* ½ cup liquid detergent, ⅓ cup baking soda, 1 gallon water. It only takes a cup of this solution in a bucket of warm water to wash a car.

- *Dish detergent additive:* When it comes to dish detergents, it doesn't pay to buy a cheap brand. You get more for your money by buying a name brand and using a coupon. If you really must buy the cheapest dish detergent, add 3 T. of vinegar to the bottle. This will help cut grease on dishes.

- *Drain declogger:* Mix 1 gal. boiling water, a cup of salt and a cup of baking soda. Pour in short spurts as drain clears little by little.

- *Roach killer:* Mix ¼-cup shortening, ⅛-cup sugar, ½-lb. powdered boric acid, and ½-cup flour. Add a little water and make into balls. Place them in dark corners where children and pets cannot get to them (behind your refrigerator, stove, washer, dryer, and in the back of your top cabinets).

- *Counter ants and insects in your pet's food bowl:* Place the dish in larger bowl that is filled with water. It will do the trick!

Bathrooms

- Two cups or so of white vinegar overnight in your toilet bowl makes any rings disappear.

- Save your soap slivers and put them in the microwave to melt. For liquid soap, add a capful or two of vegtable oil. Pour into a dispenser. Shake before each use. For bar soap, pour the soap into a smaller container and let it set until hard.

- Place a sponge on the bottom of your bar soap dish. This cuts down on the mess.

Kitchen

- Save on clean up time. When peeling or slicing anything in your kitchen, place an open paper bag or newspaper underneath it.

- Run cold water when using the garbage disposal. It solidifies the grease and flushes it away more easily.

- Store your steel-wool scouring pads in the freezer so they won't rust.

- Put your dishwashing detergent into a pump-style dispenser. You will use less and you don't have to pick up the bottle each time.

- A piece of wax paper in the microwave keeps the microwave cleaner and keeps you from having to clean it constantly.

- Place wax paper in the bottom of crisper bins in the refrigerator. You can also place paper towels underneath the wax paper for easier cleaning.

Laundry

- Create a "station" for dirty laundry, preferably right by the washer. Label the trays or bins at this station: whites, colors, dry clean, and delicate. The laundry will always be sorted when you're ready to wash! To simplify this for younger kids, keep two laundry baskets in the kids' rooms, one labeled whites and the other labeled colors. *Note:* Buy a white laundry basket for whites and a colored laundry basket for colors. Before bedtime, have each person take his or her dirty clothes to the laundry station.

- Make Friday night your laundry night. What a feeling to wake up with no laundry to do on the weekend.

- Keep hangers near your laundry area. When things come out of the dryer, hang them up immediately.

- Iron only before you wear something. If you iron it before it hits the closet, it is wasted time because it might get wrinkled before you wear it.

- Keep an ironing board always up and ready to use.

- Overloading the washer makes clothes wrinkle more, which means more work for you.

- Label your kids' dresser drawers (socks, shorts, tops, pants) so your kids can put clothes away on laundry day.

- When you fold clothes, set up a station near the dryer for each family member. They can pick up their "hot batch" and put them away.

- Why choose one laundry day per week? It saves time and wear and tear on the dryer. (The dryer is already heated up and ready to roll after the first load.)

- A clothesline is often the most simple and economical choice for drying big items like sheets, beach towels, and bedspreads.

- Hair conditioner and washcloths? Yes! Add a little hair conditioner to a washcloth, toss it in your dryer and you have a homemade "dryer softener sheet"!

- Don't throw out that ugly faded umbrella! Take the fabric off and hang it upside down from a hook. Use it as a drying rack.

- You don't need to use a whole fabric softener sheet. Cut it in half and get two loads for one sheet. Also, you can use these sheets for more than one dryer load.

- Breck® shampoo has proven to be quite effective on grease stains and blood, and it is cheaper than stain removers.

- Assign a particular towel to each family member to keep all week. A small marker dot or different colors of towels will help you know which towel belongs to whom.

Outdoors

- To clean gunky grills and oven racks put them in a black plastic trash bag on a *hot* sunny day. Pour a cup of ammonia into the bag, seal it, and leave out to cook in the sun. A hose will wipe off most of the greasy crusties.

Pets

- Buy low cost kitty litter; mix it with the more expensive clump type litter and add baking soda. (Don't ever use carpet powders to "deodorize" kitty litter. It can give your cat a urinary problem.)

7

Childhood Joys

Creating a Loving Home for Your Kids

Even though we didn't have a lot of new, store-bought toys, our childhood memories are filled with love and laughter. Having a tightwad Daddy who was handy with a hammer and saw created times of joy and just plain fun. As we grew up, our backyard became the envy of our friends because it was filled with things our Daddy created: a nice playhouse and an enormous swing set, complete with ladders and a seesaw. And we spent hours playing with the dollhouse he made for us. We decorated it with thread-spool chairs, matchbox beds, and thimble cups.

Fun and Games

- *Sticky Pick Ups:* Get pretzel sticks, bread sticks, licorice sticks, or powder candy-filled straw sticks for the kids to use to play "pick up sticks" on the kitchen table. Then they can enjoy their sweet rewards when the game is over!

• For a fun lunch, serve your children's favorite lunch items in ice cream cones and watch them munch away.

• Take some beach sand home with you in a gallon jar, color it with powdered paints and use as sand art. (Layer different colors in pretty jars, or let kids use glue to make designs on posterboard, then sprinkle on the colored sand to create pretty patterns. Wonderful for those "We are bored, Mom!" summer afternoons. This is a wonderful outdoor activity.

• Cut two holes from the sides of a pillowcase and one hole at the sewn up end and you have a perfect child-sized painting smock or an apron for helping mom or dad in the kitchen.

• Think how easy it is to make a clown face for young children. A bathing cap with "hair" (fake craft fur) glued around the edges, some makeup, and a makeshift nose (a piece of plastic with a slit cut in it works great). Happy clowning around!

> *Don't forget to let your children follow their hearts. Their dreams for their lives may not be the dreams we have for them. We've found the following to be a great formula: Common sense + Faith + Perseverance = Happy Life.*

- Glue magazine pages onto cardboard and cut into puzzle pieces for hours of fun. Old photos are great for this, too.

- Orphaned gloves and single, unmatched socks make great mini-puppets or holiday stockings.

- Create a train for your child with shoe boxes, shoestrings, and round plastic lids (for the wheels).

- A Styrofoam® egg carton is a neat 12-color paint palette for a child. Simply close the lid to keep the paint from drying out.

- Hard Styrofoam® packing can be saved to make flat forms for boats for the little sailors in your house. Complete the toy boat with straw posts and school-folder sails.

> ***Recycling Fact:*** *America uses enough Styrofoam® cups per year to circle the earth 436 times.*

- A great slumber-party project: Decorate pillowcases with fabric paint. (Stock up on pillowcases at the thrift store.)

- Water-filled spray bottles will keep your kids entertained for hours—outside of course!

- Punch the sides of postcards and lace them together to form a little box for keepsakes. (Remember the sewing cards we used to "sew" with yarn?) For a children's activity, punch holes in the cards and give your children pieces of yarn. (Wrap the ends of the yarn in tape to make "needles" to poke through the cards.) Have them creatively tie the cards together.

• Kids will love this project! The supplies you'll need are: candy pieces (Jolly Ranchers®, taffy, or dried fruit), plastic wrap, and scotch tape. Cut plastic wrap into strips 4-inches wide and slightly longer than bracelet or necklace lengths. Spread the plastic wrap on a table and place candy pieces in a line along the edge, with at least 1-inch between each piece. Carefully and tightly roll the candy and wrap into a long stick. Tape the ends together and you have jewelry! *For a more sophisticated look:* After the candy and wrap are rolled up, twist the wrap tightly between each piece of candy, forming a chain of candy.

Learning Adventures

• Make a matching game of first letters for your kids. Cut out pictures and words out of old magazines and glue onto cards. Also works for opposites and numbers.

• Cut out a design on a shoe box lid. Put in a flashlight and replace the lid for a fun way to make a light show in a darkened room. Moving the box back and forth and around increases the fun.

> *A sparkling house is a fine thing if the children aren't robbed of their luster in keeping it that way.*
> —Marcelene Cox

- Children love playing with a detergent scoop that has a small ball attached with a short string. The object is to toss the ball up in the air and catch it in the scoop. Kids can play by themselves or you can eliminate the string and they can play catch.

- Cut bagels in half, then cover with honey. Sprinkle half bagels with birdseed, tie string through hole, and attach to a tree. Then listen to your feathered friends tweet with delight!

- A two-liter bottle makes a great little fish tank if you cut off the top. Decorate with fish stickers.

- Save rectangular milk cartons for birdhouses. Cut a round hole in the side, paint, and make a stick or button roof. Add a cord for hanging in a tree.

- String cereal or popcorn on a string and hang or drape on a tree. The birds will love it—and the kids will enjoy watching!

Making Life Easier

- Blue jean pockets become an instant little carrier for kids. Add a shoestring for the handle to turn it into a purse or make two "ties" to hook on a belt or belt loops. We call these "Pocket Pals," and they can be great to use as party favors or to stuff with goodies to keep children quiet in restaurants. Filling them with Cheerios® or Gold Fish® crackers works great for toddlers.

- Keep Bibles for church and school books, as well as jackets, gloves, and boots, near front door. Also include homework or notes that have to be signed. Your mornings will go much more smoothly!

• Make school mornings less stressful! Label the rod in your children's closets: Mon., Tues., Wed., Thurs., Fri., with masking tape. Then arrange your children's complete school outfits, including socks, barrettes, and belts, on hangers in the appropriate area. You can also hang shoes in a plastic bag hung over the hanger. Older children may want to help choose their outfits, but make it clear that once they have decided for the whole week, changes cannot be made. (Unless an unexpected blizzard comes and you need warmer clothes than anticipated, of course!)

• Cookie sheets can be painted and make excellent lap trays for kids in the car. Give them an assortment of letter magnets or fun figures and they'll be happy all day. (Or at least five minutes.)

• A marshmallow in the bottom of an ice cream cone helps absorb drips for young ice cream lickers!

• Set the following guideline: No play until homework is done. Use this quiet time to get your work clothes ready for the next day, toss in a load of laundry, or to start dinner.

• Have your diaper bag ready to go at all times. Keep duplicate items in it, and you won't forget to pack anything.

It goes without saying that you should never have more children than you have car windows.
—*Erma Bombeck*

- Use nylon pants with your baby's cloth diapers. Vinyl doesn't last, and it can give the baby a bad diaper rash because it doesn't allow his or her skin to breathe.

- Hooks attached to the end of the changing table are convenient for hanging baby's wet bath towel or clothing.

- Hang a paper towel rack near the changing table. The paper towels will come in handy.

- Wicker or plastic baskets are great for toys. You can quickly throw them in, and baby can dump them out the minute you turn your back!

- Having an on-the-go lunch ready for your baby is great when baby is going to grandma's house or to the babysitter's. It's also handy when you go to visit friends. In an old lunchbox put baby spoons, a cup, a bib, a small box of cereal, crackers, and jars of baby food.

Play Areas and Living Spaces

- Any ladder painted a coordinating color makes a great place for kids to hang skates, jump ropes, hats, gloves, and coats. Hammer some nails or hooks along the sides of the ladder and on the sides of the steps to provide extra storage capability.

- An attic room makes a wonderful bedroom for a child, teen, or guest. If the attic ceilings are too slanted to position a regular bed without people knocking themselves out, put the mattress on the floor or cut the legs off the bed frame. This will work wonderfully! Kids love sleeping on or near the floor.

- Use a milk crate for a toddler swing. Cut out holes for the legs, smoothing the edges with sandpaper and adding duct tape for added protection (optional). Hang securely by a rope or chain.

- Build your child's own fun playground. Use old tires, painted barrels, beams—anything you can think of! Just use common sense and caution in thinking of safety.

Lessons from Kids

- *No matter how hard you try, you can't baptize cats.*

- *When your mama is mad at your dad, don't let her brush your hair.*

- *If your sister hits you, don't hit her back.*

- *Parents always catch the second person.*

- *Never ask your three-year-old brother to hold a tomato.*

- *You can't trust dogs to watch your food.*

- *Puppies still have bad breath even after eating a tic-tac.*

- *Never hold a Dustbuster® and a cat at the same time.*

- *You can't hide a piece of broccoli in a glass of milk.*

- *The best place to be when you are sad is in grandma's lap.*

- Use milk crates for colorful toy boxes.

- Create an easy and cheap treehouse. Position a wooden pallet in a tree and nail securely.

- Make a child's table from a regular table by shortening the legs. *Yes!* Go ahead and chop those legs off!

- Old phones are great play phones for children. Give them a pad of paper, some pencils, and a desk and they can play "office." (Great training for future executives!)

- To save space in a small nursery, don't have a separate changing table. Secure foam rubber or a heavily padded mattress to the top of a long, low chest of drawers. This provides more storage than a regular changing table, and the chest, with the mattress removed, can be used for years!

- Young children love interesting beds. A thick foam pad and lots of fun pillows make a terrific bed. Use your imagination—add a tent for a secret hide-out!

Practical Tips

- Give your kids a snack while they are doing their homework.

- Take your own candy and popcorn when you go to the movies, if the theater allows it. If not, it's much cheaper to promise the kids a treat on the way home than to pay those inflated prices for movie snacks.

- Get immunizations for you and your children free or at little cost! Most local health departments do this for free, and usually there are no income limits. They are the same shots you pay $30 for at the doctor's office.

- Mesh potato bags make wonderful bags for sandy beach toys. Dump the whole bag in water and the sand comes out of the bag and off of the toys.

- Cornstarch added to regular baby powder makes it go a long way and cornstarch is better for baby than talcum powder.

- Wrap several old phone books or old catalogs with duct tape and you have an instant child booster seat.

- An old towel can be cut to make a nifty, absorbent bib for a baby. Or cut a bib out of an old sweatshirt.

- Save empty Valentine boxes for storing precious cards or jewelry. Little girls love them for their secret treasures and notes.

- Save your crib sheets and use them to temporarily slipcover your car's backseat when you're traveling with little ones or pets.

- Make a double stroller by connecting two strollers together side by side with Velcro® strips.

- A flip-top waste can for dirty diapers is cheaper than buying a diaper pail.

- Part of the opening of a pillowcase can easily be folded over a hanger and secured with big safety pens. This can be used for a diaper holder or dirty-clothes bag.

- Baby items such as strollers and cribs are usually on sale at wonderful prices during Christmas.

- Save on baby wipes at home—use washcloths made from old towels or old cloth diapers.

• It happens before you know it. The handprints get higher and higher and then suddenly they disappear....

Supplies

• To make your own paper pulp to mold for crafts, mix cheap paper plates with water in a blender. Add water or more plates until you get the consistency you like. If you have an old screen you can press the pulp on it and let it dry in the sun. It makes beautiful, old-fashioned-looking paper stationary. Boys will love using this paper to make treasure maps!

• *Play dough:* Mix 2 cups flour, 1 cup salt, ½ cup cornstarch, 1¼ T. baking soda, 2 cups water, 1 T. cooking oil, drop of food coloring. Microwave for 4 minutes on high, and let cool. Store in an air-tight plastic container.

• *No-cook play dough:* 1 cup flour, ¼ cup salt, ⅜ cup hot water. Add food coloring if desired.

• *Gooey slime:* 8 oz. white glue, ¾-cup water, 1 tsp. borax, food coloring if you desire.

• *Silly Willy putty:* 8 oz. white glue, 2 tsp. borax, 3 tsp. water.

• *Face Paint:* Mix 4 T. cornstarch, 1 T. flour, ¾ cup light syrup, ¼-cup water, and food coloring.

Toys

• Don't buy an expensive dollhouse—make one by yourself from a bookshelf. Add walls and doors.

• Make big blocks using large brown paper bags stuffed with newspaper and taped closed. Perfect for preschool children!

- Old garden gloves can be shaped and stuffed to form a bird for a child to play with. Be sure to add embroidered eyes and a beak.

- Save broken compact mirrors for dollhouse dressers, thread spools for stools and lamps, doilies for rugs and bedspreads. Once you start thinking in miniature, the ideas are endless and your kids will love you.

- Make a shoe-box dollhouse. Use the lids for a roof, and staple together the boxes into any floor plan you want. Do you remember making these as children and the happy hours spent creating houses for your dolls? Why do we ever purchase premade dollhouses for our kids!

- Wooden spoons make great puppets. Make a face with a marker or glue on beads. Dress it up with fabric and yarn scraps. A good summertime project for kids who whine, "I'm bored!"

8

More Than Paper Routes

Marketable Skills, Job Niches, and Making Money

Our parents taught us the value of frugality and the importance of hard work, ingenuity, and getting a good education. Daddy took a lot of pride in the fact that he'd earned a college degree, and from the time we were able to write our ABCs, he encouraged us with his "university pep talk."

"To make it in this world, kids," he'd say with resolve every chance he'd get, "you'll have to get a good education." Our education was such a priority to him that even with our family's limited resources, Daddy offered to pay our tuition so each of us could attend college.

He also taught us, by example, the honor in a good day's work. In a big family, where money was far from plentiful, it really never crossed our minds not to work! As teenagers we put in our time dippin' cones behind Dairy Queen® counters, selling clothes in downtown dress shops, and cleaning up at the vet's office (as animal lovers, we even thought this was great).

As adults, during our toughest financial times—in between teaching jobs and secretarial work—Susan and I put our brains, mouths, and feet to work. One of our temporary money-making stints was to walk and deliver flyers from door to door. We felt as though we were being paid to exercise and lose some weight!

To help pay for our children to attend a Christian school, we invented our "business in a box" plan. We'd make small creations, like homemade potpourri, and sell it door to door, netting about $50 in two hours. Almost anyone can create a product for pennies, assemble it while watching TV at night or visiting with the family, then sell it during the day while the children are at school. Instant cash!

If you want something you've never had before, you're going to have to do things you've never done before. But there are plenty of programs and resources to help anyone who wants to improve his or her skills. Let's get on with our "feature presentation"—hints and tips to help you make money!

Developing Marketable Skills

Evaluating Your Situation

- If you choose to work outside the home, figure the total of your expenses, including transportation, clothing, breakfast and/or lunch at work, fast food or convenience foods for supper, child care, taxes, and social security payments. Then ask yourself, "Is my second income going to work for me or am I working for it?"

- Before you start making more money, evaluate your current spending. Do you shop impulsively, passively, or to build your self esteem? These can be severely destructive to you, your family, and your budget! (For help from someone who has been there, see Mary Hunt's books—particularly *The Financially Confident Woman*.) Will getting your spending under control alleviate the need for working outside your home?

- Don't invest in expensive office furniture. Use your imagination to create a unique office or shop with furniture you have or can pick up at a garage sale.

- Look for a job or start a business based on your talents and joys.

> *Don't forget to take some time*
> *away from stress. But don't pay to go*
> *to a gym! We have access to free exercise*
> *all around us. Take the stairs instead of*
> *elevators and escalators. Walk instead of*
> *always driving to the corner store. Use*
> *a bicycle to do Saturday errands. (Every*
> *grown-up kid should have a bicycle. It*
> *keeps you young at heart!) Don't forget*
> *to ride through a couple of mud puddles*
> *just for old-time's sake.*

- When it comes to creating a resume, fit in and stand out. Create a professional resume, but follow the rules of good business and do something a little different to stand out. For example, if you are applying for a job as a preschool teacher, create a fun colorful business card with a catchy phrase (maybe "I love little people")—something small that says, "I'm creative and unique," but not so wild that it sends a red flag to a potential employer.

- Always work smarter, not harder. Think before you leap into a business venture: "Am I making this complicated? Is there an easier way?" Keep your business organization straightforward and simple. Don't go overboard in buying supplies, equipment, and furniture.

- Make sure you check out the local and state regulations and restrictions on businesses (at home or at an outside office).

Education

- Take a tax-preparation class. You can earn plenty of money during tax season.

- The most sought after areas of employment are in the medical field—insurance records, medical assistants, nurses aids, and medical transcription, which is becoming popular for people who work at home. Sometimes crash courses in these careers are available.

Financing College

- To compare internet costs, try these resources: alt. internet.services or alt.internet.access.wanted.

- To find scholarship money for college, use the internet (www.fastweb.com). They list 180,000 private scholarships. If you don't have a computer, ask someone you know to search this out and print for you. You can also walk into the financial aid office of the college, and they will help you find a creative way to finance an education.

Helpful Organizations

- Displaced Homemakers, 1411 K St. NW, Suite 930, Washington, DC 20005.

- Entrepreneur's Business Success Resource Guide, Aegis Publishing Group, 796 Aquidneck Ave., Newport, RI 02840.

- Home by Choice is a national network of Christian mothers who have chosen to stay home with their young children and work part-time. Their newsletter, *Table Talk,* is bimonthly and costs $15 annually. It can also be used as a limited networking source. Write to Home by Choice, PO Box 103, Vienna, VA 22183.

- The Internal Revenue Service wants to help you in business. Get a copy of Publication 587, The Business Use of Your Home by calling 1-800-829-1040.

Whatever you want to do with your life, to the best of your ability try to make it happen.

- Mother and Home Books offers a rich selection of how-to books and books for inspiration on very specific work-at-home topics such as running a mail-order business. Write to them at PO Box 1228, Woodstock, VT 05091 or call them at 1-801-457-1993.

- Mothers Home Business Network offers several manuals, a newsletter called *Homeworking Mothers,* and networking with other members. Membership is $19. Write to PO Box 423, East Meadow, NY 11554 or call them at 1-516-997-7394.

- National Association for Female Executives gives materials and advice on developing and critiquing business plans. Membership costs $29 and includes a subscription to the bimonthly magazine, *Executive Female.* Contact them at 127 West 24th St., New York, NY 10011; 1-212-645-0770.

- National Association for the Cottage Industry. Membership is $45 annually and includes a subscription to the quarterly magazine *Cottage Connection,* as well as other benefits. Contact them at PO Box 14850, Chicago, IL 60614; 1-312-472-8116.

- The Small Business Administration, 1-800-634-0245.

- The *Whole Work* catalog offers a broad spectrum of books and other resources on alternative work styles. Ask for a copy from the New Careers Center, Inc., PO Box 297, Boulder CO 80306; 1-303-447-1087.

- Job Accommodation Network (information and resource center regarding rights and accommodations for those with disabilities), 1-800-526-7234 or 1-800-235-2732, http://janweb.icdi.wvu.edu.

• 9 to 5, The National Association of Working Women, Job Survival Hotline (covers workplace problems and child-care issues), 1-800-522-0925.

• If you have been laid off, here is an agency you *must* contact: J.T.P.A. This agency will send you to training schools to learn to become a cosmetologist, a nail technician, a computer programmer...the list goes on and on. They will actually pay you ten dollars per day to go to school to cover commuting cost no matter how close you live to the school. This adds up to a nice little check at the end of the month. You can find out about J.T.P.A. through your local employment office/human resource center.

Money-Making Jobs

• Have a car? Hate being in an office all day? Try delivering everything from pizza to flowers to groceries.

• Love to work outdoors and do yard work? It won't take too many yards to start making big bucks!

• Apartment buildings in safe neighborhoods are always looking for security guards.

• Begin a rental real estate empire by buying a multifamily house as your first home. You won't be sorry.

• Take a close look at ways to make money while you sleep: rental houses, investments with royalties or interest attached, renting out a bedroom, and so forth.

• Because we use so much technology in offices, technicians to repair equipment and computers are in great demand. There's also a great demand for computer data entry operators and programmers.

- Are you artistic? Place an ad offering your services for wall murals, holiday window painting, or special advertisements.

- Call real estate agents and ask them to call you the next time they need a house cleaned.

- Want to work at night while the kids sleep? Or just need an evening job? Clean offices. They're usually much easier to clean than houses!

- Look for collectibles as you rummage in thrift shops. Invest in a collectibles book and do your research. The internet is fast becoming a great source for buying and selling such treasures.

- Be brave. Open your own consignment shop or junk shop.

Money Under Your Roof!

- Start a bed and breakfast.

- Provide commercial office space (remember to check zoning regulations).

- Mobile homes are very inexpensive (especially used ones) and can be rented for income. If you have a little bit of land, divide it into lots and create a nice mobile home park. You'll make money while you sleep. You should make a profit very quickly, and in three years all your start-up expenses could be paid for. Some people even want to give their mobile home away free if you'll move it. Watch the classified ads. With mobile homes, your down payment is low to none, especially if you already own the land as collateral.

- Make money while you sleep! If you have a large home, rent out some bedrooms. If you would like to turn a room into an efficiency apartment, all it takes is a special appliance that has a stove top, small refrigerator, and sink all in one! These units costs about $400 new, and you may be able to pick up a used one. If this unit seems a little pricey, consider the following option: If you have one large room with a bathroom, all you need is a small refrigerator, hot plate (2 to 4 burners), and a microwave. The bathroom sink can double as a kitchen sink if necessary. A lot of times older people or young college students are content with this situation–especially if they can save money on rent.

Offering Services

- Care for an older person or cook for him or her. Place an ad in the paper, and have your references ready. You might even get four or five elderly people that are dropped off at your house for a weekly "day out." This could be lots of fun if you are creative and have a gift with communication and encouragement.

- You can tutor children at their homes or advertise that you do general homework tutoring at your own home. The kids can get off the school bus at your house.

- To make money cleaning houses while your kids are in school, simply place an ad in the paper.

- Like to bake, create gift baskets, or plan party food? Place an ad, meet with your new clients, then go home, bake, deliver, and accept their money! Catering is very profitable as you grow in skill and can begin targeting larger groups such as churches, schools, and civic events.

- Good at number crunching and computers? Call the offices of some of your local doctors and ask them if you can help with the medical claims billing—at their offices or from your own home.

- Are you persuasive? Call other businesses to see if they need a phone collector! You can get a percentage of money collected, and your services would be cheaper than a collection agency.

- Call a marketing research company and ask to be put on their list. They pay you to answer questions about products.

- Be a mystery shopper for companies. (Watch out, sales clerks—your next customer could be a tightwad incognito!) You can find this opportunity in local newspapers or on the internet.

Selling

- Start a flea market business: For information on what and how to sell at flea markets, write to: Flea Market Forum, 355 Great Neck Rd., Great Neck, NY 11021.

- To make extra money have a tag (garage) sale!

- Sell your used clothes, toys, small appliances, linens, and so forth to a consignment shop. The monthly check is nice. *Note:* Don't forget that there are antique shops that also work as consignment shops when you think you've happened on a good "find." Check out www.ebay.com on the internet for a huge reference page for buying and selling anything.

- If you are interested in buying rental property or you want to fix up a house for resale, know that banks will lend money with no down payment or a lower down payment if the value of the property is higher than the price you pay for it.

- If you like to sell your items at a flea market, make sure your display area looks attractive. Items should be priced three times higher than what you paid for them. You can find official flea market resources at your local bookstore or library.

- Make a craft item and sell it at a craft consignment shop. Or make holiday gifts and sell them using ads or by participating in local craft shows.

- Want to get into mail order? Choose a product to sell, place an ad that includes the price and your post office box address. When the order and money comes in, ship it!

- Don't forget door-to-door selling of cards, potpourri bags, and other items. It's fast money. Try to sell your item for less than $5. This will also help you walk off those pounds, and keep your body in good physical condition.

- One of our friends has a never-ending yard sale called "Susie's Saturday Sale." She puts out the sign when she is open, and she directs people to her garage where she has permanent tables set up. (Make garage sale or yard sale signs on fluorescent or colored paper. Make sure you use durable material. And don't forget to take the signs down when your sale is over.) Check your city's ordinances to make sure it's legal to have a permanent garage sale in your area.

- Information is the hottest selling product ever! Do you have special recipes, blueprints for unique furniture, a great party planner, or budget sheet? Sell it by advertising!

- Check into party-planning businesses like Tupperware, Mary Kay, Watkins Products, Inc., and Amway. If you have an outgoing personality and are persistent, the potential income is enormous. Here are some numbers to get you started: 1-800-MaryKay; 1-800-732-1116 (Fuller Brush); 1-800-858-7221 (Tupperware); 1-800-426-4777 (Discovery Toys); 1-800-for-Avon (AVON).

Countering Negative Thinking
with God's Promises

It's impossible.
All things are possible (Luke 18:27).

I'm too tired.
I will give you rest (Matthew 11:28-30)

Nobody really loves me.
I love you (John 3:16).

I can't go on.
My grace is sufficient for you
(2 Corinthians 12:9).

I can't figure things out.
I will direct your steps (Proverbs 3:5,6).

I can't do it.
You can do all things (Philippians 4:13).

I can't forgive myself.
I forgive you (Romans 8:1).

I'm afraid.
I have not given you a spirit of fear
(2 Timothy 1:7).

I'm always worried.
Cast all your cares on me (1 Peter 5:7).

I don't have enough faith.
I've given everyone a measure of faith
(Romans 12:3).

I feel all alone.
I will never leave you or forsake you
(Hebrews 13:5).

Piggy Banks Galore!

Keeping Up and Getting Ahead

The three Rs of saving money are: reduce, reuse, recycle. So where do you put the recycle stuff so it doesn't add to the clutter problem? All you need is one closet, or one wall of the garage, or one large shelf to put the things that may be of use later. Remember, don't save a throwaway item if you are not reasonably sure you will use it in the near future. For example, don't save every milk jug or box; just save a few. Keep your storage space simple, well organized, and labeled. Keep everything in one place, not all over the house. Use milk crates for your recycling buckets.

There's more to being a tightwad than just following the three Rs. Getting the most services for your money and negotiating the best bargains on necessary big-ticket items also plays an important role in saving money. Before we dive into finding the best bargains, checking out all the options, and discovering how small changes can save a lot of money and time, let's review some of the Bible's excellent advice regarding money:

> "You cannot serve both God and Money" (Luke 16:13).
>
> "Store up for yourselves treasures in heaven, where moth and rust do not destroy, and where thieves do not break in and steal. For where your treasure is, there your heart will be also." (Matthew 6:20,21).
>
> "Keep your lives free from the love of money and be content with what you have" (Hebrews 13:5).
>
> "The Lord sends poverty and wealth; he humbles and he exalts" (1 Samuel 2:7).
>
> "Wealth is worthless in the day of wrath, but righteousness delivers from death" (Proverbs 11:4).
>
> "Whoever trusts in his riches will fall, but the righteous will thrive like a green leaf" (Proverbs 11:28).
>
> "The man with two tunics should share with him who has none, and the one who has food should do the same" (Luke 3:11).

Now, on to more cost-cutters!

Cellular Phone Cost Cutters

- Signing up for service when you buy a car phone can save you hundreds of dollars on the cost of the phone itself.

- Until you know which phone carrier is better for you, make the shortest commitment possible.

Know the Best Plan for You

- An "economy" plan has a low monthly premium and no free airtime, so you pay extra for every minute of every call. This plan is appropriate if you need a phone only for emergencies.

- A "basic" plan has a higher monthly fee than an economy plan, but includes 30 or so "free" minutes, as well as lower rates for any extra airtime. It's designed for people who use a phone more than occasionally.

- An "executive" plan calls for a monthly fee of $100 to $200, includes several "free" hours, and has the lowest rates for extra airtime. It's best for someone who uses the phone a lot.

Credit and Tax Advice

- If you have great difficulty saving money, sign up for more tax withholding than you need. The extra will come back to you when you file your tax return.

- Save by installments. Don't stop when you reach your goal of paying off credit cards. Keep writing those checks, but to yourself, and deposit them in your savings account.

- Automate your savings and investments. Arrange for a set amount to automatically go into a mutual fund or savings account each month.

- Work your way out of a ditch of debt. Motivate yourself by making a colorful chart, checking off the payments made as you make them. For example: 20 more car payments left? Make 20 little car squares and mark off one at a time. Yes, it's childlike, but aren't we all still kids inside? And it's so satisfying to mark the last payment!

- Pause before you buy! Leave your credit cards and checkbook at home. You won't buy on impulse, and you can always go back another time and get the item. This allows you more time to decide if you really need the item.

- Get a part-time job and save the earnings.

- Pay off your entire credit card bill every month.

- When applying for a loan, the bank has amortization tables which will show you your monthly payment, length of loan, and your interest rate. Study it carefully to see how you can pay the least amount of money over the shortest period of time.

- Go for low or no annual fee credit cards.

- Use a credit card that charges a low interest rate.

- Don't pay extra for a gold or platinum card.

- Scrutinize your credit card bills. Mistakes can and do happen.

- If you need a loan, shop around for the lowest rate and the best terms.

- Pay off higher-interest-rate loans first.

- Sign up for a payroll savings plan. You will not miss this money because you never see it. It's *almost* painless.

- Make loan payments automatically from your checking account.

- Obtain six to eight weeks of free credit by buying just after the billing date and paying in full just before the due date.

- Request a personalized benefit estimate from Social Security before you need it.

Borrowing

Borrow only for necessary purposes!

Good Reasons to Consider a Loan

- buying a home

- making necessary improvements that add value to your home

- educating your children

- buying income-producing property, but only if the property produces enough income to support itself

- meeting unexpected financial emergencies

Bad Reasons for a Loan

- buying a car

- starting a business

- If you are experiencing credit problems, try to work with a consumer credit counselor before taking the drastic step of filing for bankruptcy. Credit counselors are listed in the phone book—and their advice is usually free!

- Apply for a loan at your credit union first. Credit unions often have lower interest rates than savings and loans and banks.

- Keep exact tax records.

- Prepare your own tax returns. The IRS provides many free pamphlets to help you. Internal Revenue Service, www.irs.ustreas.gov; general: 1-800-TAX-1040; forms and books 1-800-TAX-FORM, Teletax/Refunds, 1-800 829-4477.

- Call or write the IRS to request a copy of IRS Publication 17, "Your Federal Income Tax."

- Call the NFCC, National Federation of Consumer Credit Counselors (debt management program), 1-800-388-2227 if you need advice.

- Contact the Institute of Certified Financial Planners, 1-800-282-7526, www.icfp.org, if you're looking for financial planning help.

For credit reports

- Equifax, 1-800-685-1111
- Transunion, 1-800-916-8800
- TRW Credit Data, 1-800-682-7654

Homes: Mortgages, Rent, Maintenance

- Use this as a guide as typical percentages of expenditures:

    Housing 30% (includes utilities)
    Food 17%
    Giving 10%
    Entertainment 7%
    Emergency Savings 6%
    Clothing 5%
    Debts 5%
    Insurance 5%
    Medical 5%
    Miscellaneous 5%
    Savings 5%

- Ask about special government financing rates for new homeowners. There are programs you would not believe for first-time buyers. Just ask a realtor.

- Don't take out a home equity loan unless you're one of those strong people who never borrow for the wrong reasons.

- You may benefit from mortgage refinancing if you can obtain a rate at least 1.5 percent *less* than your present mortgage rate.

- Save tens of thousands of dollars in interest by taking out a 15-year mortgage or by making extra payments against your 30-year mortgage.

- Before beginning your home search, find out how much home you can afford to buy by speaking with a lender.

- If you're interested in buying a home, find desirable housing that you can live in on a rent-to-own basis—that means no down payment.

- Consider buying a townhouse for your first house. This is much more affordable and the amenities are great.

Insurance Cost Cutters

- Waive the collision damage coverage when you rent a car if your regular auto insurance already covers it.

- Take the time to learn every detail about your company's insurance plan.

- Don't waste your money on extra health insurance that covers only certain illnesses or has limited benefits.

- If your insurance agent can't find acceptable coverage for you, find an agent who is experienced with hard-to-insure clients.

- Figure out the minimum amount of life insurance you need, then work up from that figure.

- Don't jeopardize your financial future by going without needed insurance coverage.

Pennies a Day Keep Poverty Away!

- Join your employer's payroll savings plan. What you don't see you won't miss.

- Close draperies at night to keep out the cold. Open them during the day to let the sunshine in.

- Generic over-the-counter drugs are, almost without exception, just as effective as their brand-name counterparts. Generics are also less expensive.

- Be conscious of your budget when planning your wedding. Have a modest-cost wedding, and remember that extras increase the cost quickly.

- Order your checks directly from Checks in the Mail, Inc. and save up to 50 percent of the cost (800-733-4443). Also, some banks give free checking if you have automatic deposit.

- Order op-stub or duplicate checks instead of standard checks. It may cost a couple of dollars more, but you'll be able to balance your checkbook easier.

- Buy inexpensive glasses frames or even sunglasses and ask the optician to put your prescription lenses in them.

- It's winter, but don't pack away that bathing suit! Wear it with tights or leggings and turn on your local exercise show or put in an exercise tape. No need to spend money on exercise classes!

- Make your own roller suitcases by screwing rollers on the bottom of your older suitcases.

- Pay a teenager to babysit your pet while on vacation. It's usually cheaper than a kennel.

- You can spend $6 to $10 a day for lunch and snacks. That's close to $400 per month. Bring your own lunch and snacks from home if you can. Prepare it the night before and grab it in the morning.

- Pour shampoo into a pump dispenser. The kids won't use as much this way.

- College students have great garage sales and throw away a lot of wonderful treasures at the end of each semester as they pack to go home. Check it out!

- Invest in a pair of scissors that cut a nice decorative edge. Create your own stationery.

Shopping Savers

- Don't throw rebates or refund slips away—they're free money. Save all receipts, and jot down any notes on the products on the receipts. You might have to send these in to get your rebates, plus it's a good habit to save receipts in case of returns or for tax purposes. Make it a habit to cut off box tops when you're through with your products. File them away so you'll always have them when you see a rebate slip.

- If you feel a need to buy something for yourself, go to the dollar store. You will be surprised at the lift you get from buying something for just a dollar.

- Put all of your change in a jar at the end of the day. Roll the coins once a year, perhaps before Christmas or vacation time. Use the cash for special purchases or be practical and spend it on groceries or school lunches.

- Write down everything you spend for a month. Writing down what you buy will shock you to the sky, and help you control your spending.

Vehicles—Buying, Maintaining, and Using

- Keep only one car. You can take a lot of taxis for the price of owning, gassing, and insuring a second car—and you will still have money left over to save.

- *Time-saver:* Don't warm your car up in the morning. Most new engines don't require this.

- Air conditioners use up to ten percent of your car's horse-power so don't use it constantly.

- You can save up to $200 a year by following a few tips from the American Automobile Association:

—Slow down. Speeding up to ten miles per hour from 55 to 65, can increase your gas consumption by about 20 percent. Increasing to 75 mph increases it another 25 percent.

—Make sure your tires are filled to the recommended pressure.

—Close your windows to reduce air drag, thus increasing gas mileage.

—Heavy traffic times burn up lots of gas. Try to avoid driving in rush hour if possible.

—Revving up your engine not only wastes gas, it can also damage your motor.

If you need free auto advice, contact:

—AAA (Triple A) Consumer Report New Car Price Service www.aaa.com or 1-800-222-4357, 1-800-933-5555.

—Auto Safety Hotline Nationwide Auto Brokers, nhtsa. dot.gov or 1-800-424-9393, www.car-connect.com, 1-800-521-7257.

—Automobile Consumer Services, http://acscorp.com, 1-800-223-4882.

—For a free 12-page guide to used-car buying, send a SASE (legal envelope) to: How to Buy a Used Car, PO Box 1013, Maple Plain, MN 55348.

• It is our opinion that you shouldn't lease a car. It is more expensive than financing a car yourself, and leasing causes you to trade cars too often. Who needs an eternal car payment?

Financing	*Leasing* (36 mos./$20,000)
$632 X 36 months = $22,752	$380 X 36 months = $13,680
Down payment: $1,000	Down payment: $1,000
Tax (6%): $1,221	Acquisition fee: $350
Total: $24,973	Cost for lease period: $15,030
Minus rebate: $1,000	Lease-end purchase price: $10,464
Total dollar outlay: $23,973	*Total dollar outlay: $25,494*

• Avoid using rooftop carriers. They destroy the car's aerodynamics. It's like walking while dragging an elephant behind you!

- The end of September is the best time to buy tires at good prices.

- Buy radial tires. They cut your gas consumption because there is less friction than ordinary tires.

- Clean your wiper blades with vinegar and water before you buy new ones. You will be amazed at how effective this is. You might not need to buy new ones.

- August is the time to start looking for good deals on cars. The new ones are getting ready to come out, and dealers need to move the old ones fast!

- Keeping your trunk empty saves gas.

- Buy a used car in cold weather, usually January or February. This will let you see how it functions in cold weather and on slick surfaces.

Car Buying Tips

- Shop around!

- Do your homework.

- Pay cash for cars. If you can't afford it now, start saving now for your next car.

- Get into the groove of buying used cars. Why buy new when used will do?

- Research all you can before you hit the lots.

- Never finance a car over more than three years.

- A franchised dealer, one who sells both new and used cars, is a promising source for many car buyers. The dealer saves the late-model trade-ins for resale, while the less desirable vehicles are auctioned or sent to wholesalers. Franchised dealers usually have repair facilities, and they often warranty the vehicles they sell.

- Be wary of transient used-car sales operations. Many are unscrupulous dealers. Check with your local Better Business Bureau for any complaints recorded. Deal only with reputable businesses.

- Banks and other lending institutions often sell vehicles they have repossessed. Don't overlook them as a potential source of used cars.

- "As Is" means that there is no warranty on the car. You are buying a car as you see it. Any problems with the car become your responsibility as soon as you buy it. If the car breaks down or fails to perform, possibly even within minutes after leaving the car lot, it will be up to you to pay for any repairs. Most likely, your car payments will still have to be made even if the car is not running.

- Be sure you read the entire contract and understand it before you sign. Since a contract contains legal obligations, you may wish to have an attorney review it.

- Be sure you understand what Annual Percentage Rate (APR) of interest you are being charged. Check with your bank to see what reasonable rates are.

- Believe the sign, not the salesperson, when it says the car is being sold "as is." The "lemon law," being able to return a car if it constantly breaks down or fails to operate safely, only applies to new cars.

- Always find out what the dealer paid for the car and work up from that price. Automotive price directories are available at local libraries.

- Check the volume of unsold cars of the model you're seeking in *Automotive News*, a weekly trade paper. If the supply exceeds 60 days, you have much more negotiating leverage.

- Shop late in the month when salespeople are worrying about meeting their quotas, and dealers are concerned with clearing inventory.

- Shop late in the model year.

- Always compare dealership financing with the finance terms of other loan sources. (If the dealership won't give you a completed finance contract to compare with other loan sources, don't finance with the dealer.) If you own your own home, your cheapest source of financing may be a home-equity loan or line of credit rather than a new-car loan.

- Beware of add-ons once you've agreed on price. Many dealerships will try to add hundreds or thousands of dollars in useless items after you think the negotiating is over.

- Drive a hard bargain.

- Don't trade in your old car; sell it privately.

- Use an auto-buying service.

- You may get a good deal when buying a car from a private owner since no dealer mark-up is involved. However, when buying from a private owner, insist on obtaining the vehicle's service records, references, and records of original purchase. Regardless of who you purchase the car from, be sure you have thoroughly inspected the vehicle and its records prior to purchase. Have it checked by your own mechanic, if possible.

Federal Trade Commission's Used Car Rule

- If you are considering purchasing a used car, the Federal Trade Commission's used car rule may help you. Dealers must post the *Buyer's Guide* on all used vehicles. This includes used demonstrator autos, light-duty vans and trucks; motorcycles are excluded.

- The *Buyer's Guide* will state whether the vehicle comes with a warranty and, if so, what specific warranty protection the dealer will provide. The guide will also state if the vehicle has no warranty ("as is") or comes with an implied warranty only.

- The *Buyer's Guide* must reflect any changes in warranty coverage that you may have negotiated with the dealer. It also becomes part of your sales contract.

Warranties and Service Contracts

- If the used vehicle is covered under the manufacturer's original warranty, have the dealer add the following paragraph below the warranty disclosure: "Manufacturer's warranty still applies. The manufacturer's original warranty has not expired. Consult the manufacturer's warranty coverage and service location."

- Dealerships often offer car buyers service contracts, otherwise known as "extended warranties." Service contracts are not warranties; they're insurance policies. Warranties are included in the price of the vehicle. Service contracts are purchased at additional cost.

- To decide whether you need a service contract, consider several factors, including whether the warranty already covers the repairs addressed in the service contract and whether the vehicle is likely to need repairs—and the potential cost of those repairs.

- If a service contract is purchased within 90 days of buying the vehicle, warranty coverage must be stated on the contract. Federal law prohibits the dealer from disclaiming implied warranties on the systems covered in the service contract. For example, if the service contract covers the engine for six months, you automatically get implied warranties on the engine as well. This may give you additional protection beyond the scope of the service contract.

Inspect and Test Drive

- If you are interested in a specific car, ask the dealer for a test drive. Drive the car under many different conditions, such as on hills, highways, and in stop-and-go traffic.

- Ask the dealer or owner whether the car has ever been in an accident. Find out as much as possible about the car's prior history and examine its maintenance record.

- Choose a sunny day to inspect the vehicle; darkness can mask flaws.

- Bring someone who is knowledgeable about cars to assist you, if possible.

- During the inspection, note the following:

1. Look for dark stains or puddles on the pavement beneath the vehicle. If there are puddles, the car may have leaks from the cooling system, transmission, engine, or else where. With the engine cold, remove the radiator cap and look inside the radiator. The fluid should not be rusty. Greenish-white stains on the radiator indicate pinholes and leakage.

2. Body rust often lurks beneath blistered or peeling paint. Left unchecked, rust can affect the structural integrity and safety of the body and chassis. If rust erodes the car body, trunk, or floor, it can let deadly exhaust fumes inside. Wheel wells and rocker panels under the doors are especially vulnerable to rust. To check if rusted areas have been patched over with putty, place a small magnet against those areas. If the magnet doesn't stick, it may be because of a patch job. Uneven color, poorly fitted doors, trunk lid, or hood may also be evidence of an accident.

3. Check inside the trunk: A musty odor or water stains could indicate leakage.

4. A car with 25,000 miles or less on the odometer should still have its original tires. If the tires are bald or brand-new, the odometer might have been rolled back or disconnected. Unevenly worn tires may signal damage or improper wheel alignment. Check the spare tire and make sure the jack and other tire-changing gear are present. Push and pull each front tire while holding it at the top. If you hear a clunk or feel play in the wheel, wheel bearings, or suspension the joints may be worn.

5. Push down hard at each corner of the car a few times to bounce it up and down. If the car needs more than one rebound to level off, the shock absorbers are suspect. Stand about ten feet behind the car to see whether one side is lower than the other. Then do the same from the side to see whether the front or the rear sags. A lopsided car may need new springs.

6. The seats should be free from broken springs and rips in the upholstery. They should be firm, not saggy from long use. A musty odor may signal water seepage. Check out all controls and accessories. Have your helper stand outside to be sure all the lights work properly.

7. The car should start easily, even when the engine is cold. Drive-away should be smooth, with no lurching, sputtering, or odd noises. The car should accelerate smoothly and maintain power when climbing hills, depending on engine size. Pings or knocks may mean the engine needs higher octane fuel or a tune-up; leave the diagnosis to a mechanic.

8. After the engine warms, accelerate to about 45 MPH. Take your foot off the accelerator for a few seconds, and then accelerate. Your helper should be with you inside the car, watching through the rear window for exhaust smoke. Black smoke may mean that the fuel system needs adjusting. Blue smoke means that the car burns oil. Persistent, billowy, white smoke could indicate that coolant is entering the engine's combustion chambers through a blown head gasket or a crack in the head or engine block.

9. Smooth shifting is the transmission key. A manual clutch should engage smoothly, without bucking. If the transmission is automatic, warm up the engine, let it idle in park, then inspect the dipstick for the transmission fluid. The fluid should be reddish, with a faint odor of chest nuts. A dark-brown color, a rancid smell, or metal particles on the dipstick indicates trouble.

10. The car should hold the road. Steering should be smooth and precise, without much free play or vibration.

11. Have your helper kneel in the road in a safe area and watch from behind as you drive straight ahead, through a puddle, if possible. The front and rear wheels should travel precisely in a line. If the car drives at an angle, the body or frame was possibly bent in an accident. If the car's steering simply pulls to one side, a wheel alignment may save the day.

12. Accelerate to 45 MPH on a flat stretch of empty road and brake hard, without locking the wheels. In each of three consecutive tries, the car should stop quickly with no swerving, grabbing, or vibration. With the engine idling, press firmly on the brake pedal for about 30 seconds. It should feel solid and steady. If it feels spongy or keeps sinking, the hydraulic system may be leaking.

13. Cruise down a bumpy road at 30 to 40 MPH. Does the car bound, bottom out, or hop sideways? If so, the suspension could be faulty. Do you hear squeaks and rattles? They can be hard to trace. With the engine running, listen from outside the car for sputtering or rumbling from the exhaust pipe, manifold, muffler, or catalytic converter. Replacing those parts, especially the catalytic converter, can be costly.

Additional Checks

- If you are still interested in the car following the inspection and test drive, do a little more checking. To see if the car model has ever been recalled, contact the U.S. Department of Transportation Auto Safety Hotline at 1-800-424-9393. The agency will send you information about the recall. Also, take the car to a mechanic for a thorough inspection.

> *You know you're a tightwad if you
> collect your car insurance money
> and drive the dented car!*

Cutting Driving Costs

- Don't let the engine idle. Turn off the motor if you have to wait more than one minute. An idling motor uses more fuel than restarting does.

- Check into Triple A (AAA) for free traveler's checks, maps, and trip planning.

- Pump your own gas if allowed. In some areas, you can save as much as 15 cents a gallon by using the self-service pumps.

- Buy regular gas. Premium fuel provides no benefit for most cars.

- Get a second opinion on major repairs.

- Protect your transmission from careless damage. Don't allow the transmission fluid to get too low.

- Keep your cars longer than five years. If you continue driving an auto for at least two years after the loan is paid off, you could save almost enough on monthly payments to pay cash for your next vehicle.

- Choose a car that gets great gas mileage.

- Buy a tire tread-depth gauge (it's inexpensive and easy to use) and check each groove in each tire every few thousand miles. If you wait until uneven wear is obvious without the gauge, you'll have rubbed away expensive tire tread needlessly.

- If the steering wheel shakes between 50 or 55 MPH, the front wheels are probably not properly balanced. Have the wheels spin-balanced as it decreases uneven wear.

- Most fluid levels are fairly easy to check. The time it takes is well worth it. Most critical is the engine oil. Check the dipstick after the engine has been stopped at least 20 minutes. It can take that long for the oil to run down into the pan and give an accurate reading. Too much oil is not as bad as too little, but it can cause foaming and poor lubrication.

- Many batteries are sealed these days. If yours has removable caps, check the fluid level in each cell and top up with distilled water if necessary.

- Choose a manual shift. You'll save the $500 to $1,900 that an automatic transmission costs. Maintenance bills should be lower and gas mileage is better, too.

- Don't get lazy about changing the fluids in your vehicle. What water is to your body, oil and fluids are to your auto! Replace fluids yourself. Most auto-supply stores, the automotive departments of major chains like K-Mart, and even many supermarkets carry windshield-washer solvent, antifreeze, and motor oil at prices that are often less than half of what you'd pay at a gas station or a repair shop. Adding these fluids is easy.

- Change the oil filter and check other fluid levels—transmission, power steering, radiator, and brake fluid—at every oil change. Your car will need fewer repairs and last longer.

What About Price?

- Many variables determine how much a used car is worth. Prices are affected by the economy and vary in different regions of the country. The condition of the car is the most important factor in setting a price.

• Dealers need to pay overhead and provide a warranty, in addition to making a profit. Private sellers have no such encumbrances, so they may be able to sell a used car cheaper.

Sales Tax

• The sale of a motor vehicle must be documented in the state by reporting the sales price to the tax collector and paying the tax based on the price. The vehicle must be registered, licensed, and titled in the state, usually within a specified time.

• If the vehicle sells for less than 80 percent of the average "book value" for the specified model and year, you must provide proof of the actual sale price by an affidavit signed by both parties.

• The state may collect any delinquent sales tax with interest and may impose a penalty equal to twice the amount of the additional tax.

Odometer Fraud

• State laws make it illegal to tamper with, adjust, alter, set back, disconnect, or fail to connect the odometer of a motor vehicle. The odometer cannot reflect a lower mileage than the motor vehicle has actually been driven.

• An odometer reading is one accepted way of determining the dollar value and the mechanical condition of your car. Low-mileage used cars generally carry a higher price tag than those with higher mileage.

• If you suspect odometer tampering, check the following: Look for oil stickers, service records, or warranty cards showing the mileage of the vehicle. Check the physical condition of the carpet, brake pedal, seats, and any other items that might show wear. Check to see if vehicle items are in exceptionally good condition. Items in good condition might have been replaced due to excessive wear.

• Look for scratches on the odometer or the dashboard, misaligned digits, digits that stick, or an odometer that fits loosely.

• Examine the odometer statement that the current owner received when the vehicle was purchased.

• If you are purchasing the vehicle from a dealer, you should contact the previous owner to check the mileage and condition of the vehicle.

• If the dealer will not provide you the name of the previous owner, write down the vehicle identification number (VIN). This number is visible through the windshield on the driver's side. The VIN will enable you to get the previous owner's name.

Cost-Cutting on Auto Insurance

• Bodily injury liability pays for the other person's medical and rehabilitation costs. Property damage liability pays to repair or replace another person's property—a car, garage door, or lamppost, for instance.

• Uninsured motorist coverage insures you, your family, and your passengers if you're struck by a motorist with no liability insurance or by a hit-and-run driver. Underinsured motorist coverage pays your expenses after the other driver's coverage has been exhausted. In some states this coverage is mandatory, and in some states it is combined with uninsured coverage. Medical payment clauses cover doctors, hospitals, and, often, funeral bills for you and your family, regardless of who was at fault.

• Do some comparison shopping. Tell several independent agents that you're looking for a bargain without car insurance frills. Some companies offer good deals for insuring multiple items: house, car, health, and life. Get quotes from the following insurers known to have low rates: Amica Mutual Insurance (1-800-622-6422), GEICO (1-800-841-3000), Erie Insurance Group (1-800-458-0811), or USAA (limited to active-duty and former military officers and their families)(1-800-531-8080).

• Raise your deductible. On collision and comprehensive coverage you can save 15 percent to 30 percent by raising your deductible from 200 dollars to 500 dollars. Filing a small claim for, say, 300 dollars is often not a wise move because the 300 dollars may be more than offset by a rise in your insurance rate.

• Get your policy from the same company that insures your home. You may be able to save a lot on both policies.

• Coordinate personal injury protection (PIP) coverage with your health insurance. If your state has no-fault insurance laws, you can save money by agreeing that if you are injured, the first benefits will be paid from your health policy rather than your auto policy.

Organization is not rocket science. Simplify your life whenever you can!

- Consider taking a defensive-driving course. This can generate a savings of 5 to 10 percent off most coverages.

- *Multicar coverage:* Insurers say putting more than one vehicle on the same policy saves them processing costs, which most of them pass on to consumers.

- *Good driver discount:* Save 5 to 10 percent off total insurance premium as long as the driver maintains a good driving record.

- *Safety features:* You can get from 10 to 30 percent off the coverage price if your car is equipped with safety features, including automatic safety belts, air bags, antilock brakes, and antitheft devices (you must provide proof of purchase and installation).

- *Good student rates:* From 5 to 25 percent off most coverages. Generally a high school or college student must show proof of a B-average or better.

- *Student away at school:* From 10 to 40 percent off most portions of the premium. Student must live more than 100 miles from the family home.

- Get three or four insurance estimates. You'll be amazed at the wide range of costs between companies.

- Drive a "low-profile" car—one that isn't likely to be stolen or vandalized.

- Remember to ask your agent about any discounts available.

- Drop collision coverage on older cars.

"Help Me, I'm Outta Control!"

Getting Your Home and Life in Shape

Organizing! It's enough to make most women want to tear pages out of a day planner and run screaming into the night. Actually, Susan and I did get rid of our day planners, though we restrained from the screaming into the night bit. We've found it easier to use the same simple method our mother used—a nice-sized calendar hung in the kitchen that has plenty of space to write a list of activities for each day.

Two other underrated but priceless tools for today's busy woman are blank pads of paper and good writing pens—for creating daily to-do lists. (Our lists always include the subheadings "to call," "to do," and "to buy.") Perhaps because Mama encouraged us to be organized and made it fun, we actually enjoy it. Susan has won organization awards and is a whiz at whipping an office into user-friendly shape.

Like most mothers of the 50s and 60s, our Mama had a regular wash day, grocery day, baking day, and so forth. That old-fashioned method of assigning certain tasks to certain days also gives ease and structure to our lives today. On Mondays we do light housekeeping and vacuuming, we wash clothes (and our cars!) on Wednesday, and grocery shop on Friday. Though everyone's week is different, it is amazing what this simple method can do to clear your mind and guide your week.

If you go into our kitchens, we'll have to admit that we are both food filers—we organize our canned and dry goods in alphabetical order. We've also learned the value of keeping our leftovers on one shelf and dating them so we'll remember to use them as soon as possible. (Otherwise, we might end up labeling them "green," "fuzzy," "beyond description," and "gag me!")

So much of a mother's life is lived in the car, so we use a file folder in our autos to organize errands and papers. We also have a designated take-in-the-house file. We keep a "share box" in the trunk for things we want to give away. Also in the car is a box for each child, with his or her name on it, to hold school notebooks, jackets, sweaters, and sporting equipment.

Mama was a tidy lady, but her purse was a disaster area. Toothpicks sticking out of lipstick tubes, combs with bits of Kleenex and gum stuck to them. It was as if she ran out of organizational oomph when it came to keeping her purse in order. We twins, on the other hand, are fanatics about purse organization. The more pockets the better, each one serving a specific purpose. We basically have purse versions of the Swiss army knife. We could probably survive for weeks at sea or in the desert—as long as we had our purses with us.

Okay, so you aren't stranded on a desert island. But would you like help to survive the clutter and chaos of everyday life? Never fear, the Tightwad Twins are here!

> *Just when I was getting used to*
> *yesterday, along came today.*

Dressing Up; Dressing Down

- Wear tights instead of pantyhose in the winter—they are warmer and last a lot longer. Some are even cheaper than pantyhose.

- Dress up a plain vest by pinning on charms, buttons, and pins.

- Limit your wardrobe. Keep it basic and don't waste money on unmatched clothes.

- Make your teenager a "snoozin' " shirt from daddy's old shirt. Choose a white one and paint on ZZZs.

- A black velvet ribbon and a charm or button makes a great choker necklace.

- Make your own bridal veil with veiling material, white ribbons, faux pearls, and a hot glue gun! Research the look you want in bride magazines and start creating.

- Touches of gold or silver add instant elegance to a plain outfit.

- A gold or silver chain at the hardware store can look great as a necklace. Add some charms.

- A matching scarf or piece of fabric in a blazer pocket can add a touch of class and extend your wardrobe tremendously.

- A tiny touch of animal print adds class to a purse (tie on a scarf), a belt (roll a scarf around it), earrings, and shoes (use clip-on animal earrings).

- You probably know that dry cleaning costs can slowly bleed you dry. Five dollars per week equals $260 per year. Avoid buying garments that have to be dry cleaned.

- For handkerchiefs, cut off ends of old ties and use the large ends or the small ends for your blazer pockets.

- Vests are professional looking and much cheaper than blazers. Reversible vests are a double savings.

- All cream and all black always looks expensive and tasteful.

- Square-shaped iron-on patches can be cut into cute shapes and placed on T-shirts, jeans, and other pieces of clothing. Also use on purses and hats.

- Watch for a pretty girl's lace collar at a garage sale or thrift store and use it interchangeably on different dresses. This goes for your dresses, too.

- Oversized shirts and sweaters look great with leggings. Hit the thrift stores.

- Fake rhinestones are the next best thing to the real thing! And who really knows?

- Gold and silver shoes can make most outfits look dressier.

- Denim hats can be embellished with flowers, buttons, earrings, and pins.

- Wear three to five necklaces at a time with a black dress for a touch of elegance.

- Buy inexpensive men's white undershirts or T-shirts and let your kids paint them.

- If you have a limited budget, choose neutral colors for your basic wardrobe pieces. Add color with pocket scarves, shoes, purses, and earrings.

- Put pantyhose in the freezer overnight before wearing them. This helps them resist runs. (And gives your kids and husband an interesting conversation piece to talk about when they reach for the ice cream.)

- Lost an earring back? Use a small cut-out piece of plastic (from deli containers, notebook cover, etc.) or an eraser to hold the earring in place.

- String your own necklaces with inexpensive beads or use beads from a necklace that has broken.

- Cut off the sleeves and shoulders from worn or stained shirts and blouses—and they become dickeys.

- Add thin rubber sole guards to your new shoes so they'll last longer. Great for children's shoes.

- Change your clothes right away when you get home from work. You will feel more relaxed with your family and save wear and tear on your good clothes.

Home Organization Simplified

- Keep your life simple. Have one box for all receipts, one box for warranties, and so on. Keep them all in one place—a closet, a desk, or in your home office. (Hat boxes, stacked, make great decorative receipt catchers. Use a different box for each year.)

- When moving, leave your clothes in the dresser drawers.

- Use towels to cushion breakable items. Use towels also to store breakable items.

- Do certain jobs in certain months. When the season changes, wash windows, check fire alarms, clean out closets, and so on.

- Spend 15 minutes before bedtime straightening every room in the house. This makes the morning much easier to handle.

- Put all appointments on *one* family calendar near the phone. Too many calendars create confusion.

- Keep a cute basket on the dining table filled with napkins, paper plates, forks and spoons, salt and pepper, and so forth. Refill it every week or so.

- *Make serving a cinch:* Serve food from the stovetop or kitchen counter in buffet fashion. Clear a spot on the counter for cups, ice, and pitchers of iced tea or water. This way of serving is so much faster and easier for everyone. The time you save hauling plates and pots back and forth to the table can be spent sitting and visiting with the kids once they've served themselves in the "kitchen cafeteria" line.

- We often think paper plates are a great buy for quick sandwiches and lunches. They are cheap and save a lot of work.

- Your crockpot is your private cook when you are away from home. Use it for everything you can think of. *Note:*

Don't forget the hot bread trick: Wrap bread in aluminum foil (may butter ahead of time), place it on top of a crock pot lid that has been placed on the pot upside down. Your meal not only will be done when you get home, but your bread will be hot until you serve dinner. (Someone's gonna love you for this trick, admire your organizational skills, and—because it was easy for you—your good mood!)

• Fitted sheets and comforters really save time when making the bed. Pin the bottom of the comforter with a huge diaper pin that blends in with the decor of your comforter. When you make the bed, the comforter will at least be where you can just toss it up easily and not in a pile on the floor!

• Buy or make pillow shams instead of using pillowcases in a child's room. Put the decorative side up for daytime, flip it over for bedtime.

• If you use regular dishes, fill the sink with sudsy water and have the family rinse and deposit their own dishes in the sink after they're finished eating.

Keeping Jobs Simple and Cheap

• Garlic added to outside plants keeps bugs and worms out of your containers and your garden.

• Wet sewing thread and run it over a bar of soap to make it easier to thread the needle.

• Sew on a four-hole button as if you were sewing on two buttons. If the thread breaks on two of the holes, you have a backup system.

• Slip a rubber band over the clothesline and use to hold a hanger in place.

• Fasten a length of chain to the end of a clothesline and to a hook on the post. You can tighten the line by just using the next link of chain.

• Tired of guessing how much mail weighs and how many stamps to put on it? Five quarters and a ruler make a pretty accurate postal scale. Lay the pencil on a flat table or counter and put a 12-inch ruler across the pencil, centering it on the 6-inch mark. Stack five quarters on the 3-inch mark and center the letter you need to mail on the 9-inch mark. If the letter outweighs the quarters, you need to add more postage. Five quarters weighs exactly one ounce, which is the weight of a one-stamp letter.

Making the Most of Your Time

• Use your kitchen timer for deadlines to help kids start and finish a given chore. It is much more fun to "beat the clock." This works for adults, too—there's still a little bit of kid in all of us!

• Always keep blank paper or work to do in your car so you can be productive when you encounter those waiting times—waiting for your child at a game, waiting in line at the bank, waiting for your turn at the doctor's office.

• Use your answering machine or caller ID as your personal phone call screener. Don't be chained to the phone.

• Keep a tray or flat box containing lunch items in the refrigerator. This facilitates "assembly line" lunch making.

- Consider hiring a teenager to help with dishes, laundry, and general housekeeping. They usually work cheap, and you can keep your sanity.

- Keep a pad and pen next to your bed. Scientists say our most creative thoughts come to us just before we nod off and as soon as we wake up.

- Keep a notepad for list-making in your purse.

- Attach your keys to your purse so you won't have to spend time looking for them.

- Change purses only when you dress up. (This will be easier if you keep your makeup in a small container so it can be switched in seconds.)

- When you get your new calendar, mark all important dates, such as birthdays, ahead of time. Also, pencil in any jobs you need to do that month, such as spring cleaning. Write in all of your appointments you know in advance: dental cleanings, vaccinations needed, vacations, and graduations.

- Saying yes to everything, making your goals too big, and not being willing to delegate not only wastes your time, but you'll be behind before you know what happened!

- Remember, your time is valuable. Leave some "margin" for life's interruptions and the people you love.

Stolen Spaces and Packing Materials

- Blow air into plastic sacks and close them with a twist tie. Use them to pack your glassware. This cushions them when you are moving or storing them.

- Put winter blankets under your mattress during the summer. This saves on storage space and keeps the blankets clean.

- Use an old side of a crib and place it upright on its end for hanging towels and wash cloths. (Also makes a nice drying rack for bathing suits and hand-washables.)

- Hang hooks under shelves, behind doors, and inside cupboard doors. This can really save space.

- Hang a broom or mop handle from the top closet rod. Make sure it hangs at least two feet below the rod. This creates a space-saving lower rod for more clothes.

- Old or unused suitcases that can be slipped under the bed are wonderful for storage.

- Beds that have under-the-bed drawers are great for saving space in tiny bedrooms, and they make great storage for toys, sheets, and miscellaneous items.

- By stacking older, narrow coffee tables, you can create some great storage for your garage.

- Window seats are wonderfully space efficient. They provide storage and places to sit.

- Ottomans or stools with lift-off tops are great for storage.

> *"Never lend your car to anyone to whom you have given birth."*
> —*Erma Bombeck*

- Keep three boxes in the bottom of every child's closet (yours too!) labeled: *store* (memory items and certificates), *sell*, and *share* (give away).

- Keep a small box in each bathroom and in the kitchen for cleaning items. This saves time and space.

- Slip old drawers under the bed to store items. They even have handles. Why not paint them to match the room's decor? They also make great toy bins.

- Need to utilize the changing table for something besides changing the baby? Use the bins of the changing table for toys such as blocks, coloring books, and crayons.

- Buy items that have multiple uses. For example, trunks can be used for coffee tables as well as storage.

- Coffee tables have quite a bit of space underneath. Quilts can be folded and displayed, or you can store your family photo albums there.

- Army cots can make easy beds for company (especially kids and teens) and are easily stored under a bed.

- Indoor and outdoor foldable chairs are great to have on hand. Buy them at yard sales.

- Invest in those mini-appliances that go on top of your kitchen counter or under your cabinet. Most are more efficient and work just as well as larger appliances.

- Hang up everything you can in the garage: Bikes, lawn chairs, folding chairs, ladders, and lawn tools.

- A seldom used closet can sub as a pantry.

- Flower pots are cheap organizers that come in a variety of colors and sizes.

- Hang wooden pallets or "forklift flats" on the wall. Then, using hooks or nails, hang your pots, pans, and cooking utensils.

- Don't underestimate the convenience of using stacked milk crates for storage.

- Large trash bags hung over hooks on a garage wall make excellent recycling stations. (Remember, though, that many stores will not accept returnable aluminum cans that have been stored in plastic sacks.)

- Nail old blue jean pockets onto a board as an organizer. This is not only a great idea in the house and garage, but what a wonderful idea for the kids' rooms.

- A beat-up old dresser is great for storage. Put it in the garage or in a closet. Label the drawers.

- Simple shelves can be made by stacking concrete blocks and boards. Use these in your garage or a closet to keep and reuse.

- Use that muffin tin to hold plastic cups filled with storage nails, screws, and office supplies. For smaller items use the tin without the cups. *Note:* Tins can be painted any color you like. Works great in drawers.

- Use empty tissue boxes as dispensers for plastic bags.

- If you are taking a hanging clothes bag on your trip, hang your toiletry bag on the hanger too. This saves suitcase space.

• Ask your grocery store for any display shelves they may be tossing out. Some are great for storing items, especially in your garage.

• Hanging wire baskets are great for storage. Hang each basket alone or in multiples on a chain or rope.

• Cover any cardboard box with fabric, old maps, or decoupage them with paper for use anywhere in your house.

• The wall space going up the stairs makes a great photo gallery.

• Under stairs there are usually huge spaces for storage. Think about opening up the stair wall and installing some shelves or cabinets.

• Tables, especially card tables, are excellent space-saving items. Use the space underneath, then cover the table with a long tablecloth.

• Consider hanging linens and tablecloths in your closet if you are short on drawer space or shelves.

• Use small square boxes or little green strawberry or fruit boxes to store fragile pieces of dinnerware such as china cups.

• Use any container you have on hand to hold pencils, envelopes, and rubber bands. You can use tin cans, plastic cups, vases, plastic containers, or baskets.

• Use old suitcases for photos or for storing larger office items such as paper. They also work great for storing children's artwork or special papers.

- Fabric and ribbons can make an ugly storage box new again.

- Old record album covers are great for storing flat items—school papers, odd-sized art, and big photos.

- Baskets are so cheap at thrift stores and yard sales. They come in all shapes and sizes and are great for organizing any space or filling with a variety of goodies for gifts.

- Look at everyday objects as organizers. Cutlery trays can turn into desk drawer organizers or dividers for nuts and bolts.

- Hanging shoe bags are an organizer's dream! You can use them:

    —as an office organizer.

    —a bath toy organizer to hang in the tub area. Poke some holes in each pocket for drainage.

    —to organize and store your tools in the house or garage.

    —to keep food molds and cake decorating supplies handy.

    —for jewelry and rolled up belts storage.

    —to organize your shoes

Vehicles Organization

- Keep your car emergency items stocked: a small fire extinguisher, "call police" signs, first aid kit (homemade), a blanket, a jug of water, jumper cables, a whistle, and pepper spray to name a few. It's best to always be prepared.

- The warm sun makes your ashtray a wonderful aromatic holder in your car if you put a little potpourri in it.

• Keep a few plastic bags in the car for garbage. This makes it easier to keep the car clean and to make sure the garbage gets thrown away.

• Keep clean cookie sheets in the car for your children so they can do their homework or artwork on their own "car desks." Also makes a nice lap tray for drive-through meals.

• Clean out your car on a set day of the week.

• A T-shirt over a bucket seat and headrest in a car makes an instant protective seat cover/cooler.

• A plastic shower curtain or tablecloth in the trunk of your car comes in handy if you have to kneel down to change a tire or check under the car.

• Your driving time will go much smoother if you pack a permanent car "busy box" for children or grandkids. Include: coloring books and crayons, plastic toys, cassette player with headphones, cassettes, activity books, sticker books, picture books, and a pillow and blanket. Change these things once a month for variety.

• Keep envelopes, snacks, rubber bands, paper, stamps, tape, and scissors in your car. You will be amazed at how often you will need these items. A folding or collapsible camping chair is also wonderful to carry in your vehicle if you have room.

> *I don't have time to take it one day at a time anymore. Now I need two or three.*

11

Checking Out the Bargain Bin

Our Favorite "Best Buys"

"New" was simply not done in our family. Not if there was a "used" alternative, that is. We never owned a new car. ("Drive it off the lot and you've already lost a thousand dollars," Daddy would say.) Daddy was always dragging home a "treasure" that he'd found or someone had given him so we had lots of surprises, just not the store-bought variety. Our seamstress Mama made all of our clothes for us as we grew up, she even sewed our beautiful prom dresses out of satin and lace. We did have to purchase shoes, but we knew if Mama or Daddy could have figured out a way to make these for us as well, they would have tried! (And Mama did cut the toes out of dress shoes and tennis shoes to make us her home-made version of sandals.)

Today Ann and I (Susan) rarely buy new items, especially if they are not on sale. Once we realized the savings of buying almost-new at rock bottom prices, it's hard to bring ourselves to pay full price again. Now we find ourselves shopping at thrift stores about 90 percent of the time, even for household items. Not only does this save money, but we get the thrill of the bargain hunt as well.

However, we must admit there are times when only new will do. So we put our twin heads together, read consumer magazines relentlessly, and asked for opinions concerning common purchases. We came up with a list of what we personally judge are the best buys. Remember, this is only our opinion, combining all information available to us through a variety of resources. It is a gift to you, our readers, with love from us—the Tightwad Twins. May we present..."The Best of the Best Buys!"

Air Conditioners
House

1. Carrier 42KB009101/38KB009101
2. Hitachi RAS-3098U/RAC-3098UV
3. Mitsubshi MS09EW/MU09EW

Room

1. Panasonic CW-606TU
2. Sharp AF-505M6
3. Kenmore (Sears) 75055

Batteries
Alkaline AA size

1. GE/Sanyo GES-AC2AA
2. Radio Shack 23-552
3. Ever Ready Energizer E91

Heavy-Duty AA Size

1. Rayovac 5AA, Mallory M15SHD

Alkaline C Size

1. Duracell MN1400, Sears DieHard 93902, Rayovac 814

Alkaline D Size

1. Duracell MN1300, Ever Ready Energizer E95
2. Sears DieHard 93903, Rayovac 813
3. GE/Sanyo GES-AC2D, Panasonic AM-1PA

Rechargable AA and D size

1. Radio Shack Millenium
2. Radio Shack Hi-capacity 23-149
3. B2C Hi-capacity 12-140

Blankets, Electric

1. J.C. Penny Odyssey
2. Sunbeam 3/8 Heated Fleece
3. Slumberrest All Seasons

Boom Boxes

Large

1. Aiwa CA-DW550 and Sharp GX-CD610
2. Panasonic RX-DT610
3. JVC PC-X130

Small

1. Panasonic RX-DS15

2. JVC RC-Q50

3. Aiwa CSD-EX30u

Cameras (Compact 35mm)
Long Zoom Range, Autoexposure

1. Nikon Zoom-Touch 800

Medium Zoom Range, Autoexposure

1. Fuji Discovery 1000 zoom

Single Focal-Length Lens, Autoexposure

1. Yashica T4

Single-Focal-Length Lens, Fixed Exposure

1. Kodak Star 835AF

Can Openers

1. Oster 556-11 or 3121

2. Black & Decker EC43

3. Betty Crocker BC-1104

Electric Under-Cabinet Models

1. Hamilton Beach Spacesaver 76400

2. Black & Decker Spacemaker EC60G

3. Black & Decker HandyOpener KEC160B

Carbon-Monoxide Detectors

1. Nighthawk 2000 (A great buy!)

2. Enzone Air-Zone II

3. Pama GHD-2010

Car-Safety Seats

1. Century 590 series
2. Evenflo Travel Tandem series
3. Century 565 series
4. Evenflo Joyride Convertible series
5. Century 560 series

Cellular Phones

1. Audiovox MVK-500
2. Fujitsu Pocket Commander
3. Motorola Micro TAC Lite
4. Blaupunkt TC-132
5. Antel STR 1300

Clothes Dryers

We have found that KitchenAid, Whirlpool, Maytag, and Kenmore (Sears) need fewer repairs than other brands.

Cordless Phones

1. AT&T model 4615
2. GE model 2-9615
3. Panasonic model KX-T3960

Dehumidifiers
Large Capacity

1. Whirlpool AD0502XA0
2. Kenmore (Sears) 5550
3. Emerson Quiet Cool DG60G

Medium Capacity

1. Whirlpool AD0402XA1
2. GE AHD40SSS1
3. Kenmore (Sears) 5541

Small Capacity

1. GE AHD25SSS1
2. Kenmore 5525 (Sears)
3. Whirlpool AD0252XA1

Fire Extinguishers

Full-Floor Multipurpose Models

1. Buckeye 5HI SA-40 ABC
2. Ansul Sentry SY-0516
3. General TCP-5LH

Large Multipurpose Models

1. Ansul Sentry SY-0216
2. Kidde FA 110 G
3. Fyr Fyter D1A10

For Flammable Liquid and Electrical Fires

Large

1. Ansul Sentry SY-0236
2. General CP-21/2J
3. General CP-5J

Meduim

1. Kidde FA 5 G
2. Fyr Fyter 210D

Small Models

1. Kidde KK2
2. Kidde PKG 200
3. Fyr Fyter PKP 100

Freezers

A freezer can actually cause you to waste money if you don't manage what you freeze prudently. Our readers like KitchenAid best.

Garage Door Openers

1. Stanley ST200 Standard
2. Sears Craftsman 53325
3. Chamberlain 2100 Standard Duty
4. Stanley ST400 Deluxe
5. Genie G8000
6. Sears Craftsman 53425

Heaters, Portable Room

Baseboard Models

1. Holmes HBH-500
2. Patton FL-60
3. Patton FL-40A

Fan-Forced Models

1. Heat Stream 29H40
2. Windmere HH-3122
3. Holmes HH-970A

Ceramic Models

1. Toastmaster 2517
2. Holmes HCH-4066
3. Del-Rain 1500V

Liquid-Filled Models

1. Delonghi HM-15
2. Duracraft CZ-600
3. Delonghi TYP3107

Radiant Heaters

1. Heat Stream 30H50
2. Lakewood QT-1
3. Toastmaster 2465

Humidifiers

Console Models

1. Toastmaster 3435
2. Emerson HD14W1
3. Bemis 4973

Tabletop Models

1. Duracraft DH-904
2. Duracraft DH-831
3. Toastmaster 3408

Microwave Ovens

As a rule, Panasonic has fewer repairs.

1. Samsung MW6430W
2. Sharp R-3A66
3. Admiral (M. Ward) KSA-8551A

Refrigerators

For overall performance, we have heard good things about Amana, Kenmore (Sears), and KitchenAid refrigerators.

Large Top-Freezer Models

1. Whirlpool ET25DKXD
2. Kenmore 65571 (Sears)
3. GE Profile TBX25PAX
3. Amana TR25S5

Small Top-Freezer Models

1. Kenmore (Sears) 65971
2. KitchenAid KTRP18KD
3. Whirlpool ET18HTXD

Saber Saws

1. AEG BSPE 100X
2. Metabo EP565
3. Hitachi CJ65V2

Shavers, Electric

Men's

1. Norelco 985RX
2. Norelco 885RX
3. Braun 4504B

Women's

1. Panasonic ES271W
2. Panasonic ES205WC
3. Norelco WS600

Shopping, General

Clothes

We also give twin salutes to the places that sell new "classy clothes for less cash."

- Ross
- K-Mart's Jaclyn Smith collection
- Wal-Mart's Kathie Lee collection

Dollar Stores

We give our best twin salutes to the Dollar General Stores—we adore them! Most of the following items can be found in these stores (and more!). We love this chain because of its variety of items as well as its prices. Food items such as mashed potato mix, juices, soft drinks, applesauce, snacks, soups, and boxed candies are usually available at reasonable prices. Here are a few of our "best buy bargains" on smaller everyday items; some are priced (approximately) and some are just listed to help you realize the great gift items that this store has available. (All are ridiculously reasonable and all in one place on one floor!)

makeup

hairspray

shampoos

deodorants

perfumes

framed prints

school supplies

greeting cards ($.50)

flannel shirts ($5)

sweatshirts ($5)

pants ($5)

toys ($10 and less)

paper products

bakeware

small appliances (can openers, toasters, mixers) ($8.00)

brooms, mops ($1)

wallpaper borders

lamps ($10 or less)

steelwool soap pads, 15 ($1)

dishwashing detergent, 5 lbs. ($2)

lemon-scented bleach, gal. ($.75.)

liquid detergent for dishes, 64 oz. ($1)

abrasive cleanser, 3 ($1)

fabric sheets, 40 ($2)

spray disinfectant ($1.50)

window cleaner, 64 oz. ($1)

pine cleaner, 64 oz. ($1)

baking soda ($.50)

potpourri sprays ($1)

mildew remover ($2)

rug cleaners ($1)

storage boxes ($1)

houseshoes ($2)

quilts

throws ($10)

mats

towels

shoes

baby items

flowers

ties, great looking ($3)

pantyhose

underwear

jogging outfits ($17.50)

reading glasses ($5)

Christmas gifts and decorations galore!

18 function knife ($3)

flashlights ($1)

mittens ($1)

Gifts

Our most favorite drug store is Walgreens because of the wonderful selection of inexpensive holiday gifts—everything from trinkets to toys and at very affordable prices. Twin hoorays for Walgreens!

Groceries

Our last "best buy" winners for bargain grocery shopping in our areas are Winn Dixie and Kroger. Their generic deals are fantastic and are more plentiful than any other chain, in our opinion. *Don't forget:* Shop in a lower-priced neighborhood, but not one that is unsafe.

Our second choice chains are Sav-a-Lot, Aldi's, and Gulley's (surplus groceries). These are great for teeny-tiny budgets. (Believe us—we know about teeny-tiny budgeting....)

Showerheads, Low-Flow

1. Teledyne Water Pik Original Shower Massage SM-62-P
2. Teledyne Water Pik Original Shower Massage SM-82-W
3. Pollenex Power Shower PS320

Smoke Detectors

1. First Alert Double System SA301
2. Dicon Photoelectric 440
3. First Alert Photoelectronic SA203

Steam Irons

1. Philips Azur 80
2. Sunbeam 3956 (A great buy!)
3. Oster 3993

Stoves
Electric Ranges

As a rule, a smooth-top range performs no better than a conventional model. Smooth-top ranges sell for around $600, but price tags between $700 and $900 are more common. Compare that with prices of $300 to $500 for a typical conventional range. We recommend Whirlpool because of its history of few repairs. Next in line are General Electric, Hotpoint, Frigidaire, and Kenmore.

Gas Ranges

Think twice about choosing one of the cheapest gas ranges—or one of the priciest. The best values in gas ranges are between $600 and $800.

Toaster Ovens and Broilers

1. Black & Decker T660G

2. Toastmaster 336V

3. DeLonghi XU-20L

Toasters

For the most part, relatively small differences separate the better models. All the following are #1 with us:

1. Oster 3826

2. Sunbeam 3824

3. Krups 118

4. Maxim ET-9 (A great buy!)

Toilets, Low-Flow

1. Gerber Ultra Flush 21-302 (A great buy!)

2. Kohler Trocadero Power Lite K-3437

3. Kohler San Raphael Lite K-3394

Tools

Power Drills
Corded Models

1. Bosch 1001VSR

2. Bosch 1000VSR

3. Makita 6402

Cordless Models
1. Sears Craftsman 27139
2. Porter Cable 9852
3. Ryobi TFD170VRK

Cordless Screwdrivers
1. Sears Craftsman 11124
2. Black & Decker SD2000
3. Black & Decker SD3000

TV/VCR Combinations

13-inch sets	*19- and 20-inch sets*
1. Sharp 13VT-F100	1. Goldstar GCV1924M
2. Goldstar GCV1324M	2. Samsung CXB1922
3. GE 13TVR40	3. Hitachi 20VR2B

Vacuum Cleaners
Uprights
1. Sharp Twin Energy EC-12TWT4
2. Hoover Power Drive Supreme U6323-930
3. Kirby G4

Canisters
1. Nilfisk GS90
2. Miele White Pearl S434i
3. Eureka Excalibur 6975A

Vehicles
Compact Cars

1. BMW 325i
2. Honda Accord
3. Infiniti G20
4. Mazda 626
5. Mercedes-Benz 190E
6. Mitsubishi Galant
7. Nissan Stanza
8. Suburu Legacy
9. Volvo 240 Series

Minivans

1. Dodge Caravan/Plymouth Voyager
2. Ford Winstar
3. Mercury Villager/Nissan Quest

Sport Utility Vehicles

1. Chevrolet Blazer
2. Ford Explorer
3. Jeep Grand Cherokee

Subcompact Cars

1. Ford Escort/Mercury Tracer
2. Geo Prizm/Toyota Corolla
3. Honda Civic
4. Mazda 323 Protogé
5. Nissan Sentra
6. Saturn

Best Choices for Women

1. Buick LaSabre
2. Chevrolet Lumina
3. Dodge Plymouth Neon

4. Ford Taurus

5. Honda Accord

6. Mitsubishi Galant

7. Nissan Maxima

8. Pontiac Bonneville

9. Saturn SL

10. Toyota Camry

Washing Machines

1. KitchenAid

2. Whirlpool, Hotpoint

3. Sears, Maytag

4. Amana

5. General Electric, Speed Queen

6. White-Westinghouse, Frigidaire, Magic Chef

12

Resources

Finding Help Quicky and Economically

Free Pamphlets and More

- The Consumer Information Center (CIC) is an excellent information center for booklets published by many Federal agencies. Topics include financing a house, understanding how Medicare works, finding jobs, homework helps, cutting the cost of car insurance, and many more. There are over 200 free booklets. (Other booklets may be purchased for a small fee.) Send your name and address to: Catalog, Consumer Information Center, Pueblo, CO 81009.

- Decorating Ideas Booklet—send $.25 to Decorating Ideas Booklet, Georgia-Pacific Corp., 900 SW Fifth Ave., Portland, OR 97204.

- Health and Beauty Booklet—Health & Beauty Booklet, c/o Castle and Cooke Foods, Box 7758, San Francisco, CA 94119.

- Free ruler/bookmark—send request and a self-addressed stamped envelope (SASE) to Union Label Dept., ILGWU, 1710 Broadway, New York, NY 10019.

- Laundry tips—send for "The Way We Wash Our Clothes," Dow Brands, Dept. 180, PO Box 78980, New Augusta, IN 46278.

- Catalog of free publications—thousands of free publications available just for the cost of shipping. Write to Cooperative Extension Service, Michigan State University, East Lansing, MI 48824.

- Easy to Make Gifts—Johnson's Wax, Consumer Service Department, Racine, WI 53401.

- Consumer Reports will send you a free issue of *Consumer Reports* magazine and a copy of their buying guide (1-800-234-1645).

Cooking

- Free cookbook—Wholegrain Cookbook, Quaker Oats, Box 14077, Baltimore, MD 21268.

- Meat information—educational material on the raising of meat animals and meat preparation, American Meat Institute, PO Box 3556, Washington, D.C. 20007.

- Recipe book for chicken, beef, and fish from Lea and Perrins Worcestershire sauce—Free Recipe Book, Lea and Perrins, Fairlawn, NJ 07410.

- Twenty-four best recipe books from Best Foods: For a list of these books, write to Best Foods, Dept. LL, Box 307, Coventry, CT 06238.

- Velveeta cheese recipes: Velveeta Cookbook, Box 633, South Holland, IL 60473. Write "Cheese Recipes" on envelope.

- Campbell's Soup Recipe Book, PO Box 1232, Bensalem, PA 19020. Ask for recipes and send a SASE.

- Great pasta recipes everyone will love. Send a business-size SASE to Mueller's Endless Pastabilities, PO Box 307, Coventry, CT 06238. Ask for the recipe book.

- How to get the most food for your money—write to College of Agriculture and Home Economics, Office of Information and Aids, 2120 Fyffe Rd., Columbus, OH 43210.

- Microwave cookbook, 32-pages—send $.50 to Reynolds Wrap Kitchens, Box 6704, Richmond, VA 23230.

- Microwave Cheese Recipes, Wisconsin Milk Marketing Board, 8414 Excelsior Dr., Madison, WI 53717.

- Dole's Quick and Easy Recipes, PO Box 7758, San Francisco, CA 94120. Send a SASE.

- "Bake-a-Bread" booklets, Fleischmanns Educational Services, PO Box 2695, Grand Central Station, New York, NY 10017.

Family Help

- Active Parenting Covenant House, 1-800-825-0060, 1-800-999-9999.

- American Association of Retired Persons Medicare Hotline, www.aarp.org, 1-800-424-2277; www.hcfa.gov, 1-800-638-6833.

- American Counseling Association/National Association of Child Care Resource, www.counseling.org, 1-800-545-2223, Referral Agencies 1-800-570-4543.

- Eldercare Locator Information/Referral Line National Council on Aging, 1-800-677-1116, www.ncoa.org, 1-800-424-9046.

- Family Therapy, www.adopt.org/adopt; www.aamft.org, 1-800-374-2638, 1-800-862-3678.

- Hospice Education Institute, Hospice Link, 1-800-331-1620.

- Parents Without Partners, 1-800-637-7074, parentsplace.com.

Housing

- You can get a 119-page booklet that provides information on over 100 housing programs offered by HUD. Call 1-202-708-1420 and ask for the booklet "Programs of HUD," or write to Department of Housing and Urban Development, Washington, DC 20410-4000.

Medical

- You can really save with some mail order drug companies:

  Diversified Prescription Delivery, PO Box 787, Waterville, ME 04903-0787, 1-800-452-1976.

  Medi-Mail Inc., PO Box 98520; Las Vegas, NV 89193-8520, 1-800-331-1458.

  Family Pharmaceuticals, Box 1288; Mt. Pleasant, SC 29465, 1-800-922-3444.

- Get the "Free Guide to Drugs, Medications, and Cleaning Products," a 272-page booklet. Write to Bristol Myers Company Guide to Consumer Product Information, Box 14177, Baltimore MD 21268.

- What can you do about family living costs? Write for a free book from the Office of Information, Cooperative Extension Service, Ohio State University, 2120 Fyffe Rd., Columbus, OH 43210.

- Student Guide–Federal Financial Aid Programs (Item 513), Consumer Information Center, Dept. MB, Pueblo, CO 81009.

- Financial Planning, Especially for Women (a free 21-page booklet written by money columnist Grace Weinstein). Write to Financial Planning, American Council of Life Insurance, 1001 Pennsylvania Ave., NW, Washington, D.C. 20004.

- Refund and Coupon Info: Tropicana Products Consumer Center, PO Box 338, Bradenton, FL 34206. Write on envelope: Refunding for fun and profit.

- "Ways and Means Handbook" is full of money-making ideas for clubs or organizations. Send $.50 to Sperry and Hutchinson Co., Consumer Services, 2261 Brookhollow Plaza Dr. #207; Arlington, TX 76006.

- Avoid 15 of the most common money blunders that people make—write to AETNA Life and Casualty, Attention Public Relations Department, 151 Farmington Avenue, Hartford, CT 06156.

Safety

- U.S. Consumer Product Safety Commission (regarding unsafe products and products recall), 1-800-638-2772.

Traveling

- Call American Youth Hostels at 1-202-783-6161 for inexpensive vacation lodging. Also check out the vacation exchange club at 800-756-HOME.

- You can relive those dorm days! For a small fee, you can stay in dorm rooms when students take their vacation breaks. Sometimes these rooms go for good bargain prices. Call 1-800-525-6633 for detailed information.

13

The Best Bargain of All

A Gift for You

If we were allowed to share only two secrets for surviving hard times they would be to lean on God's promises, and learn to laugh. Our parents taught us how to do both.

Mama grew up in a Christian home. Her faith, though quiet, was deep and real. So much was conveyed without words, even her peaceful acceptance of her cancer diagnosis. She was one of those women who adored babies and indulged her affection for God's fresh-born creations by taking charge of the church nursery. Little did we realize that our tenderhearted mother, who loved cuddling infants, would not live long enough to see her own grandchildren. The joyful birthdays of our own babies were tinged with some sadness that Mama wasn't able to hold them, coo at them, and rejoice with us in all their "firsts."

We remember our Daddy praying at meals and leading family devotions. Our family attended church an average of three times a week. We don't remember it any other way, but our big brother and sister tell us it was not always like this. There were years when Mama would walk the children to church each Sunday while Daddy stayed home. Then, one Sunday, one of us kids began to feel ill so Mama had to turn us around and walk back home. To her great surprise, Daddy took the three kids who were feeling well down the street and into church. His first time in church alone.

He came home that afternoon and announced that he'd prayed to accept Christ and had been baptized—and that was that. You could have knocked our mother over with a feather duster, but she was thrilled.

Daddy presented God as an authority to be obeyed; Mama taught us that God was also a dear Friend and Guide. All in all, we ended up with a pretty balanced view of God (or as balanced a view as two unbalanced sisters can get!). Ann often laughs that I (Susan) will not get on an airplane until I have physically touched it and prayed over it. Then I spend the rest of the flight trying to balance the plane by leaning left and right with my body. We believe that faith is often coupled with a hearty sense of humor and a realization that none of us is perfect.

The Lord's Baseball Game

Bob was caught up in the spirit where he and the Lord stood by to observe a baseball game. The Lord's team was playing Satan's team. The Lord's team was at bat, the score was tied zero to zero, and it was the bottom of the ninth inning with two outs. They continued to watch as a batter stepped up to the plate whose name was Love.

Love swung at the first pitch and hit a single, because Love never fails.

The next batter was named Faith, who also got a single because Faith works with Love.

The next batter up was named Godly Wisdom. Satan wound up and threw the first pitch; Godly Wisdom looked it over and let it pass, because Godly Wisdom does not swing at Satan's pitches.

Ball one.

Three more pitches and Godly Wisdom walked, because Godly Wisdom never swings at Satan's throws. The bases were loaded.

The Lord then turned to Bob and told him that He was now going to bring in His star player, Grace.

Bob said, "He sure doesn't look like much!"

Satan's whole team relaxed when they saw Grace. Thinking they had won the game, Satan wound up and fired his first pitch. To the shock of everyone, Grace hit the ball harder than anyone had ever seen. But Satan was not worried; his center fielder, the Prince of the Air, let very few get by. He went up for the ball, but it went right through his glove and hit him on the head, which sent him crashing to the ground. The ball continued over the fence for a home run! The Lord's team won.

The Lord then asked Bob if he knew why Love, Faith, and Godly Wisdom could get on base, but could not win the game. Bob answered that he did not know why.

The Lord explained, "If your love, faith, and wisdom had won the game, you would think that you had done it by yourself. Love, faith, and wisdom will get you on base, but only My grace can get you home. And My grace is the one thing Satan cannot stop!"

God's love is free to all and does everyone good that it touches. But we are mindful that it cost God's Son His life to offer us an invitation to eternity filled with that love. It is our prayer that those of you reading this book discovered ways to save money and enjoyed a few laughs along the way. But our biggest hope is that you'll accept the best deal you'll ever get in this world—the offer to embrace God's gift of grace (unearned love) as your own. No coupons required, and the warranty is beyond incredible. We think you'll be amazed, as we are, what a little grace can do in an ordinary life.

The Story of the Cracked Pot

A water bearer in India had two large pots; each pot hung on one end of a pole which the man carried across his neck. One of the pots had a crack in it, while the other pot was perfect. The perfect pot always arrived full at the end of the long walk from the stream to the master's house; the cracked pot arrived only half full.

This daily trek continued for two full years. Of course, the perfect pot was proud of its accomplishments, fulfilling the task it was created for. But the poor cracked pot was ashamed of its flaws, miserable that it fell short of perfection.

One day the flawed pot spoke to the water bearer of its sadness. "I am ashamed of myself, and I want to apologize to you."

"Why?" asked the bearer.

"I have only been able, for these past two years, to carry half my load because this crack in my side causes water to leak out all the way back to your master's house. Because of my flaws, you have to do all of this work, and you don't get the full value for your efforts," the pot said.

The water bearer felt sorry for the old cracked pot, and in his compassion he said, "As we return to the master's house, I want you to notice the beautiful flowers along the path."

Indeed, as they went up the hill, the old cracked pot took notice of the sun warming the beautiful wild flowers on the side of the path, and this cheered it some. But at the end of the trail, it still felt a pang of sadness, because it had leaked out half its load, and so again it apologized to the bearer for its failure.

Then the bearer asked, "Did you notice that there were flowers only on your side of the path, but not on the other pot's side?" The pot nodded. "That's because I have always known about your flaw, and I took advantage of it. I planted flower seeds on your side of the path, and every day while we walk back from the stream, you've watered them. For two years I have been able to pick these beautiful flowers to decorate my master's table. If you were not created thus, my master would not have had this beauty grace his house."

Each of us has our own unique flaws. We're all cracked pots. But if we will allow it, the Lord will use our flaws to grace His Father's table. In God's great economy, nothing goes to waste.

So as we seek ways to minister together, and as God calls you to the tasks He has appointed for you, don't be afraid of your flaws. Acknowledge them, and allow Him to take advantage of them, and you, too, can be the case of beauty in His pathway.

> *Go out boldly, knowing*
> *that in our weakness we*
> *find God's strength.*

About the Authors

Ann Fox Chodakowski lives in Brandon, Florida, with her husband, Alex. Ann raised her two children alone for many years before remarrying. She holds an MA in Education and taught school for 15 years. She lives in a small-but-organized townhome and is a list organization nut. Even so, she will always believe that Susan is the cheapest twin!

Susan Fox Wood lives in her hometown of Paducah, Kentucky, with her husband, Steve, and daughter, Holley. She lives in a turn-of-the-century home that she bought without a down payment—and renovated it herself! Susan holds an associate degree and has received several awards on office management and organization. She learned the art of "tightwadery" during ten years of being a single parent. She admits she is thrifty, but believes Ann is most definitely the cheapest sister. And that's the truth!

You've seen them on television, heard them on the radio, and read about them in magazines....The Tightwad Twins have three main talents: They are twins, they are tightwads, and they can talk, talk, talk! The twins want to share with you hundreds of money, time, and organization tips mixed with a little nonsense and nostalgia just for fun. If you would like them to speak at your church, organization, or other group, contact them at:

foxtwin2@aol.com

or write to them at

Tightwad Twins
PO Box 1331
Brandon, FL
33509-1331